Baths
of Diocletian

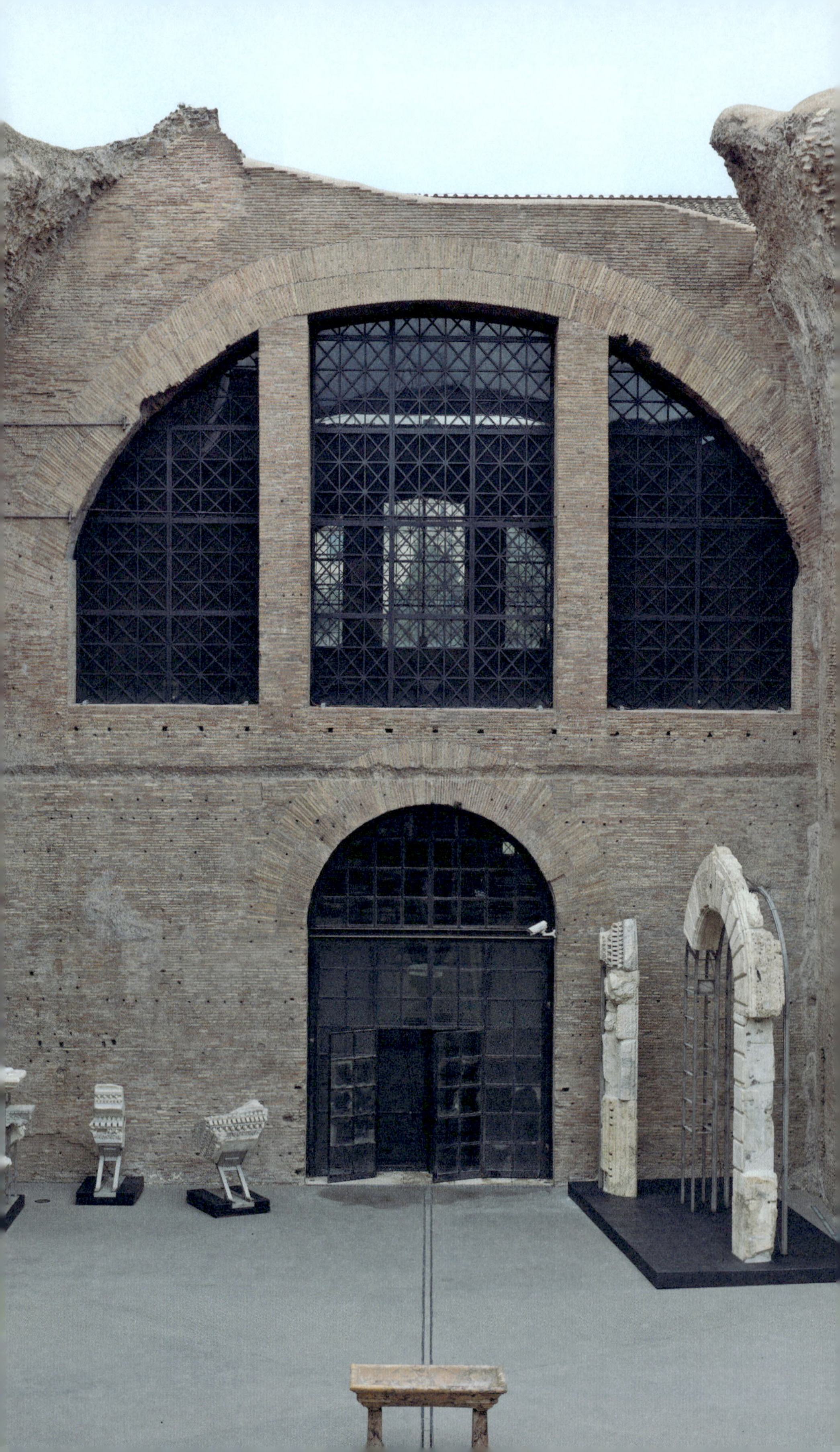

·baths· ·of·diocletian·

guide

Ministero per i Beni
e le Attività Culturali
e per il Turismo

Museo Nazionale Romano

Electa

Facing title-page
Hall VIII; at the back
Hall V.

Texts by
Claudio Borgognoni (C. B.)
Matteo Cadario (M. C.)
Carlotta Caruso (C. C.)
Anna De Santis (A. D. S.)
Nunzio Giustozzi (N. G.)
Marina Magnani Cianetti (M. M. C.)
Marina Piranomonte (M. P.)

Photograph Credits
Archivio Fotografico
del Museo Nazionale Romano
Giorgio Cargnel
Romano D'Agostino
Luciano Mandato
Simona Sansonetti

Reprint 2019
New Update Edition 2014
First edition 2011

Published by
Mondadori Electa S.p.A., Milano

www.electa.it

Contents

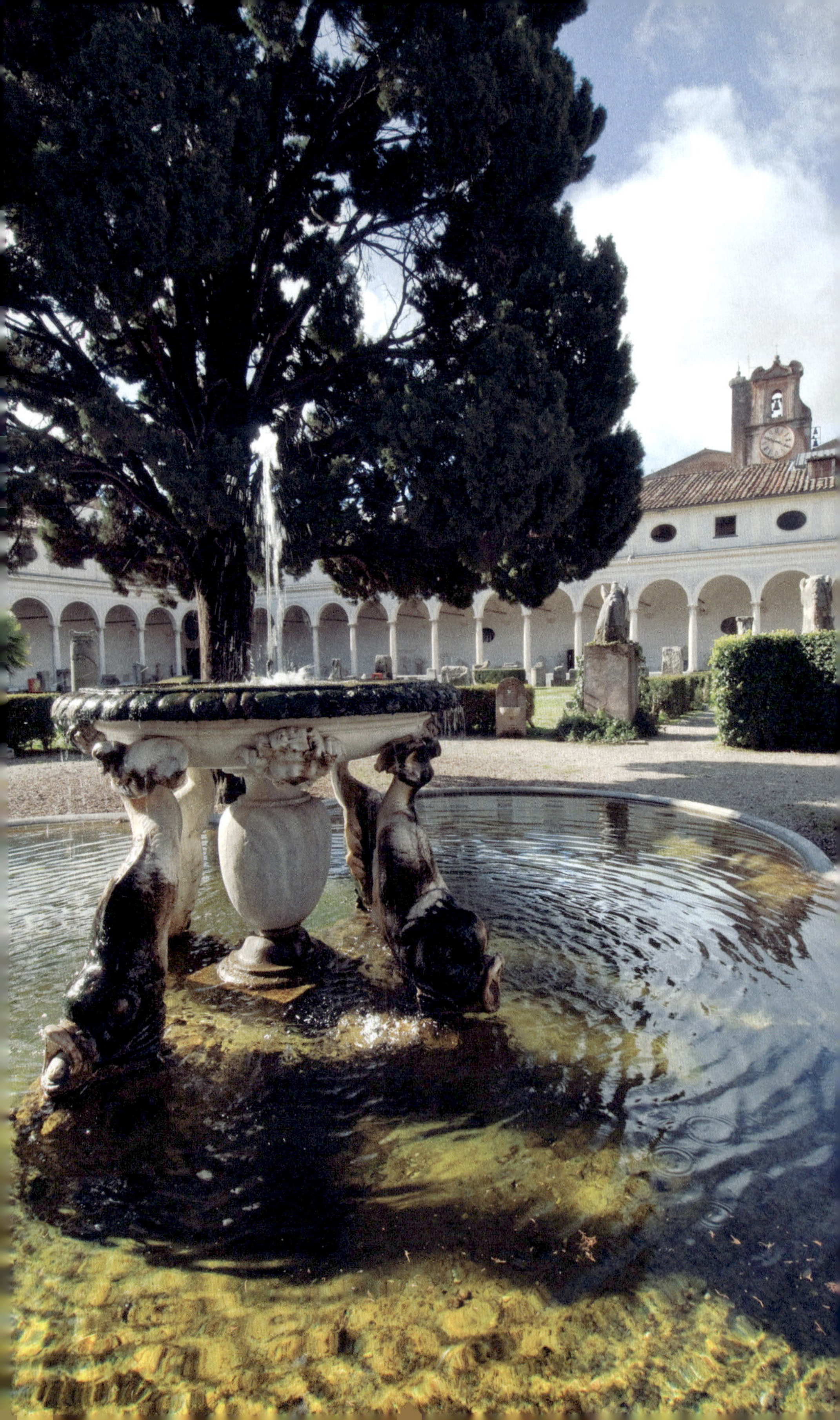

Baths of Diocletian

The Baths of Diocletian, the largest in the ancient Roman world, were built in just eight years, between 298 and 306, on a flat area between the Viminal and Quirinal hills. A large number of both private and public buildings were demolished to build the complex, as witnessed in the dedicatory inscription (see p. 59). The Baths covered an area of more than 13 hectares (some 32 acres), contained in a vast enclosure, with the main entrance on the north-eastern side and, in the middle of the opposite side, a large exedra with steps corresponding to today's Piazza della Repubblica. On both sides of the exedra there were two libraries, flanked at the extremities by two circular halls; one of them was transformed in 1598 into the Church of San Bernardo, while the other is still visible at the beginning of Via del Viminale. The main halls of the *frigidarium*, *tepidarium* and *calidarium* were aligned along a central axis; all the other halls were placed symmetrically around this axis. On the sides of the *frigidarium* were placed two large outdoor gymnasiums, the western one of which is partially visible in the archaeological area of Via Cernaia. Two octagonal halls were aligned with the *caldarium*. One of these was used as a planetarium from 1928 until the 1980s.

The complex was restored at the beginning of the 5th century AD and maybe used for a few more decades. Cited in various versions of the *Mirabilia Urbis Romae* ("Marvels of the City of Rome", a guide intended for pilgrims travelling to the city), the Baths still retained much of their original decorations in the Renaissance, as shown by numerous artists' drawings dating from the 15th and 16th centuries. After almost a thousand years, in 1561 Pope Pius IV decided to build a basilica in the internal area of the Baths, consecrated to Our Lady of the Angels, with an attached Charterhouse, to commemorate the Christian martyrs who, according to the legend, died during the construction of the Baths. Michelangelo, commissioned to design the church, used both the *frigidarium* and the *tepidarium* areas without altering the original structures and planned the main cloister. During those years the small cloister adjacent to the church's presbytery was built, and it occupies about a third of the *natatio*'s surface. Starting from 1575, with Pope Gregory XIII, several halls of the Baths were converted into warehouses to store grain and oil.

The last significant changes to the complex took place after the Italian capital's transferral to Rome. Following the dissolution of the congregation of Carthusian monks, who definitively abandoned the Charterhouse in 1884, the area around the Baths was involved in large-scale town-planning interventions. As well as the construction of the Roma Termini railway station, the zone also became home to the Ministry of the Economy, the Grand Hotel, Palazzo Massimo, Piazza dell'Esedra, with the large buildings by G. Koch following the old exedra and destroying certain sections of it, and lastly Via Cernaia, which definitively separated the western gymnasium from the remains of the external enclosure, the latter still being visible along Via Parigi. In 1889, the complex of the Baths of Diocletian and the Charterhouse became the site of the National Roman Museum. (C.B.-C.C.)

Michelangelo's Cloister, the central fountain.

Hall IX of the Baths.

Reconstruction of the plan of the Baths of Diocletian complex.

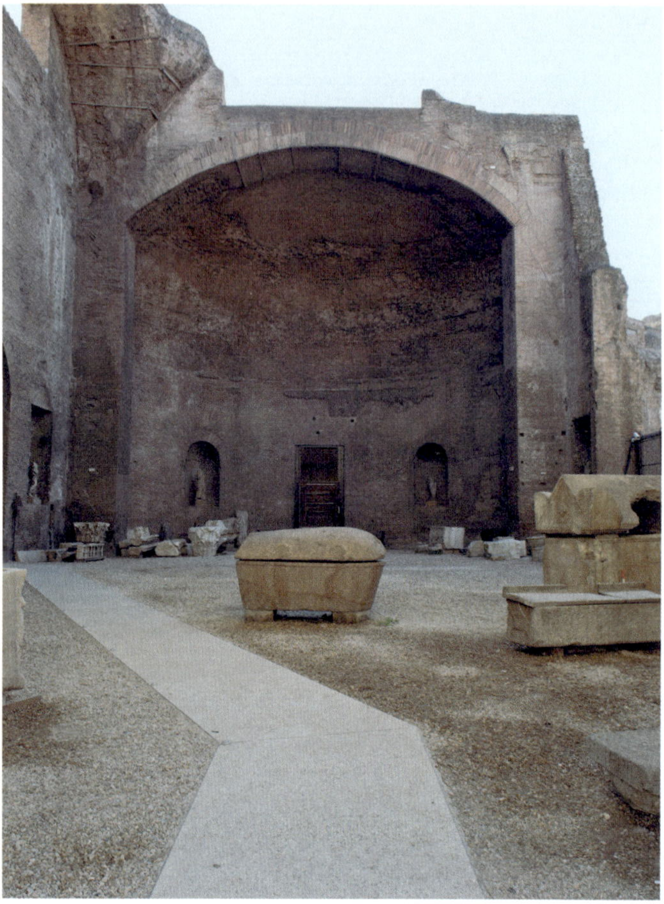

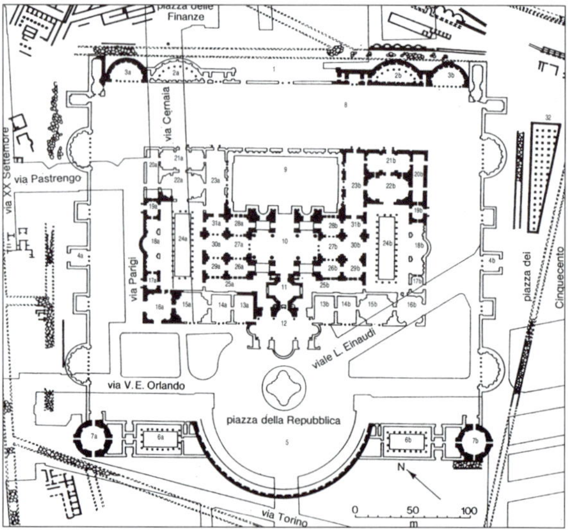

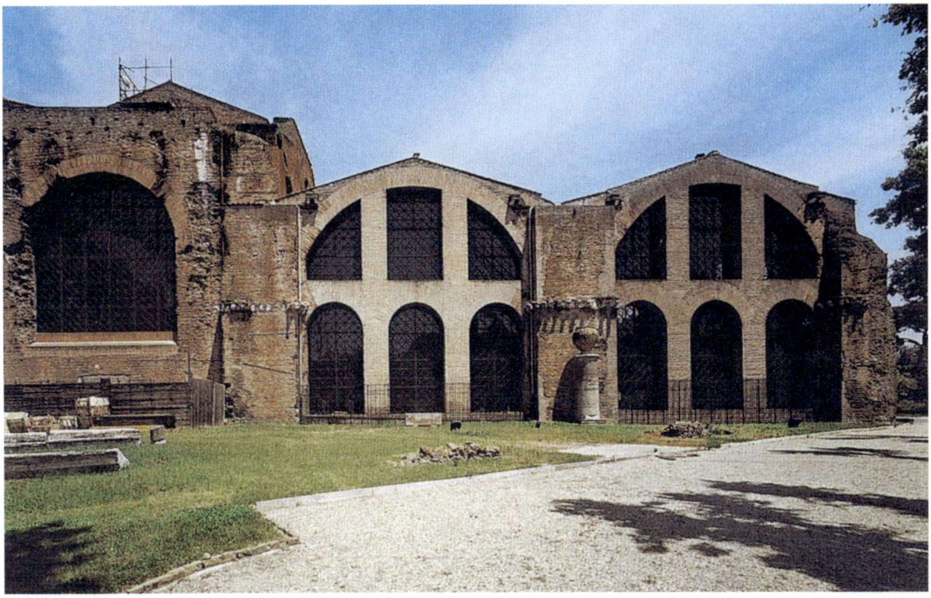

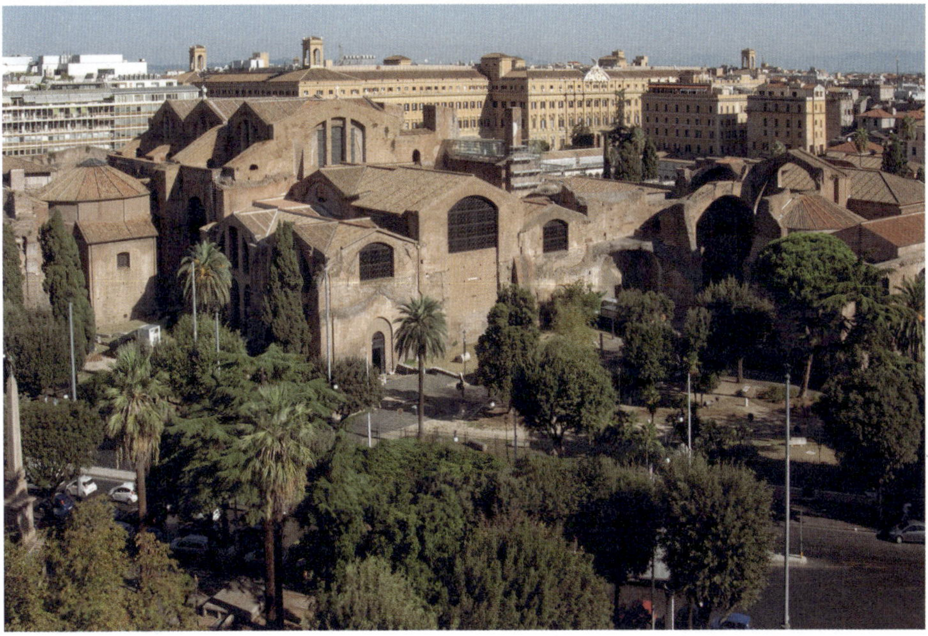

External view of the halls located between the *frigidarium* and the southeastern gymnasium.

The Baths of Diocletian today.

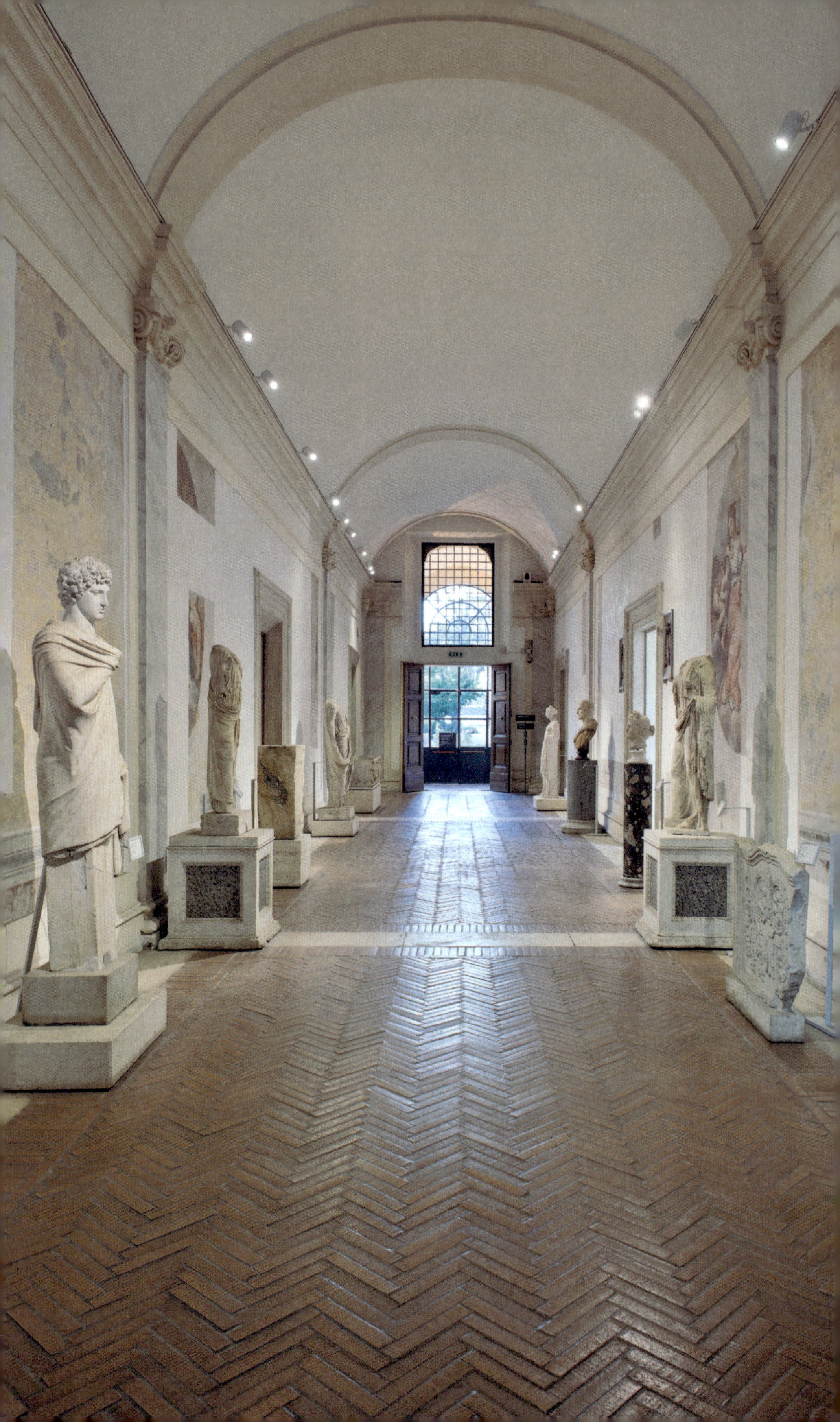

The Garden and Entrance Hall

Since the foundation of the National Roman Museum in 1889, the Garden has been set aside for the display of numerous archaeological finds originating from Rome and its suburbs, datable between the late 1st century BC and the 3rd century AD. Inscribed funerary altars are arranged to the sides of the Garden's entrance, among which there is the remarkable altar of *Valgia Silvilla*, with a representation of the gates to the underworld on the rear. Statues of togaed figures are displayed along the path leading to the museum, together with several architectural elements (columns, capitals and architraves) originating from various ancient buildings. The central fountain is dominated by the imposing volume of the colossal krater, which was already used as a fountain in ancient times, although its original placing is unknown. It is a rare artefact with only one other comparable example in Rome, the krater in front of the Basilica of Santa Cecilia in Trastevere. The fountain is surrounded by large inscribed funerary altars dedicated by relatives or heirs to senators, soldiers, foreign figures, a freedman of Caligula and the patron of a rich freedwoman. The path on the right is lined with funerary cippi and steles in travertine of various origins, including funerary steles dedicated to soldiers of different corps stationed in Rome and to the Imperial German Bodyguard. Sarcophagi and funerary statues are displayed in front of the museum entrance.

The museum's entrance hall corresponds to the old corridor of the Charterhouse that led to Michelangelo's Cloister. On the walls, one can see parts of frescoes which emerged during the restoration, attributable to Giovanni Odazzi (1663-1731) and portraying the Theological Virtues. A sarcophagus is displayed on the right-hand side originating from the area of Santo Stefano Rotondo, portraying a Dionysian procession composed of centaurs, satyrs and maenads, while on the opposite wall one finds a statue of Aphrodite dating from the 2nd century AD inspired by a Greek model from the 5th century BC. This is followed by a post-antique bust inspired by the so-called Capitoline Brutus. At the entrance to the Epigraphic Museum stands the funerary altar of *T. Flavius Felix*, an archivist in the office in charge of the arrival and distribution of marble from the quarries of Luni. (C.B.-C.C.)

The Entrance Hall.

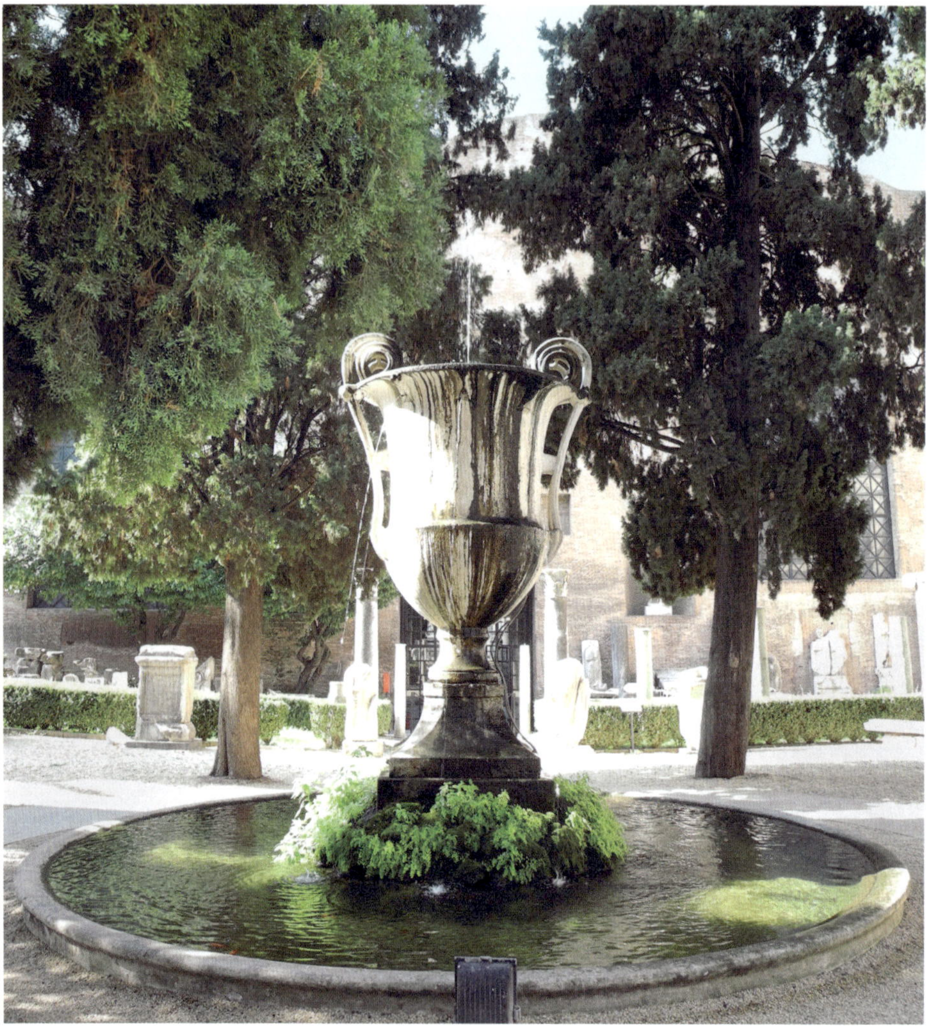

Krater-fountain at the centre
of the 16th-century Garden.

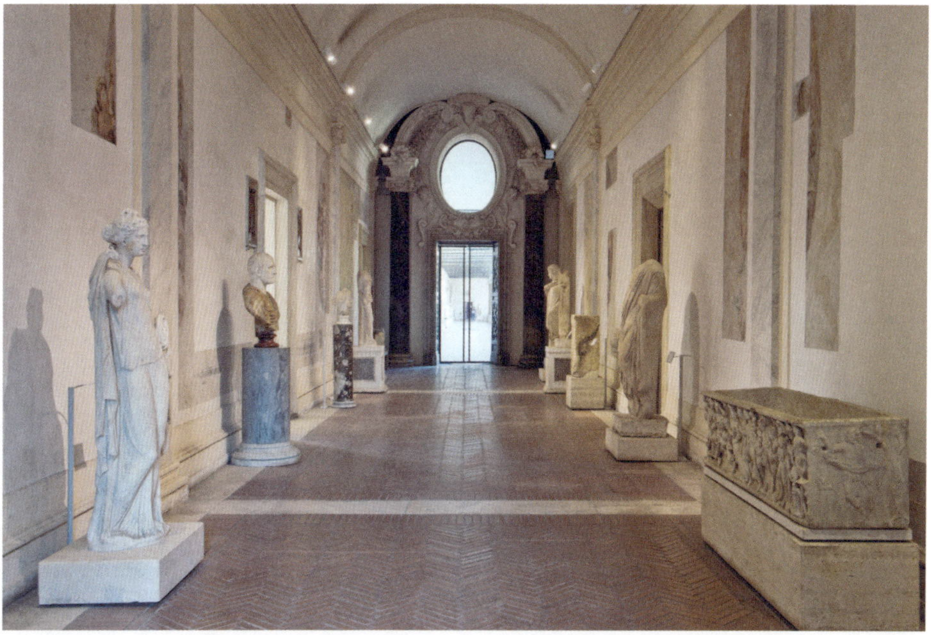

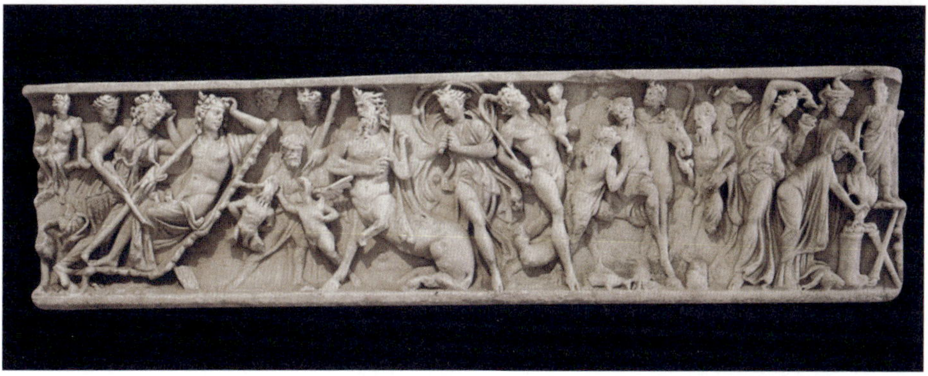

The Entrance Hall.

Sarcophagus with Dionysiac procession.

Page 14
Funerary altar of the scribes of the curule aediles Q. Fulvio Prisco and Q. Fulvio Fausto.

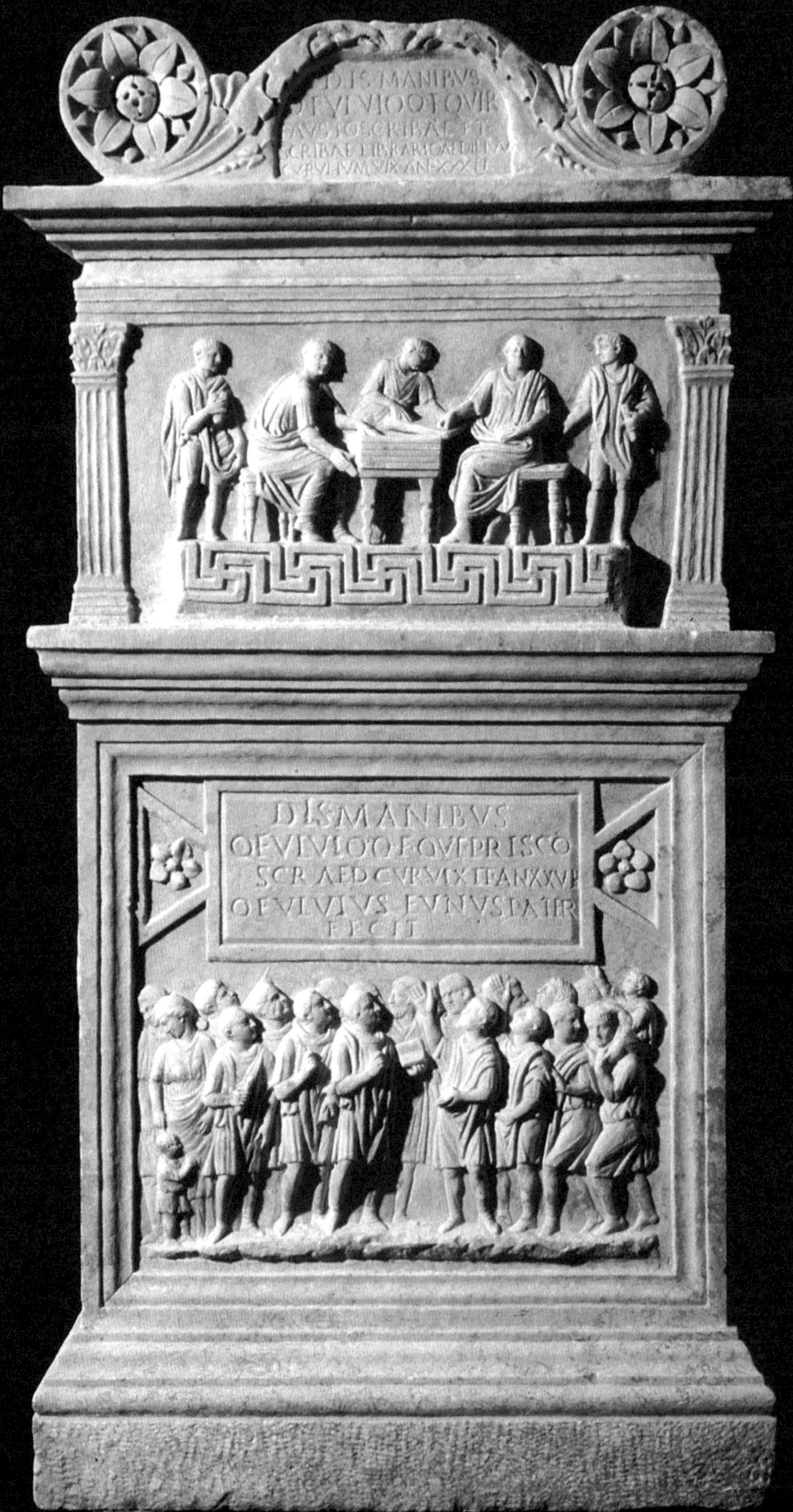
DIS MANIBVS
Q FVLVIVS EVNVS PATER
FECIT

The Epigraphic Museum

The National Roman Museum houses one of the most important and richest collections in the world, with a total of some 10,000 inscriptions. It was established from historic collections, such as the one from the Museum Kircherianum, and from the great public works undertaken in the construction of Rome as the national capital. It continues to be expanded today with materials discovered throughout the territory of Rome. Exhibited on three floors of the museum are around 900 items which illustrate social, political, administrative, economic and religious aspects of the Roman world. In addition to the inscribed message they bear, the epigraphs also provide indirect information which can be grasped from the analysis of the document in its entirety.

By opting to entrust one's message to an epigraph – a means of communication addressed to the community – the author chose the technique to be used and the support on which to write according to the message itself.

Rooms I, II, III, IV

Room I presents the various forms of written communication used by the Romans, showing us the authors of the inscriptions, their contents and the practical aspects of their execution. *People who write* (the emperor, a slave's slave, a man in love, a mother, a cook, a musician, a cobbler, a baker); *what they write* (a dedication, the dedicators' names, the name of a licensee of a water concession, an artist's signature, a hallmark, an occasional graffito, a curse); *how they write* (with a mould, a graver, a mosaic, a brush or scratching). The exhibited documents include a particularly interesting fragment of the *forma Urbis* from Via Anicia – a map of Rome dating from the 1st century AD representing the Temple of Castor and Pollux in the Campus Flaminius area – and the sepulchral inscription of *Claudia Florentia Secundina*, on the back of which the stonecutter noted down the draft of the text to be inscribed.

Room II is dedicated to the earliest examples of writing. Appearing in Latium on funerary objects dating from the 8th to 7th centuries BC, and usually composed of the name of the addressee or the donor only, they document the introduction of the Greek alphabet and its gradual adaptation to the sounds of the Latin language. The oldest evidence of writing in the Greek alphabet found in Italy comes from Gabii; it is inscribed on a small vase discovered in a woman's tomb at the Osteria dell'Osa necropolis. The interpretation of the inscription, in Greek characters, is uncertain. Reading from left to right, it is possible to recognise the Greek word *eulin*, "one who spins thread well", or *eunin*, "bed, tomb", or less likely *euoin*, a Bacchic cheer. Reading from right to left, the Latin expression *ni lue*, "do not steal", is recognisable. The Praenestina brooch (here a gold cast from the original conserved in the Pigorini Museum) dates from the 7th century BC and is considered the oldest document of the Latin language. Its authenticity has been demonstrated by recent chemical and physical analysis as well as by linguistic data. The formula employed is that of the "speaking object", as if the object itself were speaking. It attests that *Manios* the goldsmith or the donor made *–fhefhaked–* the brooch for *Numasios*. During the 6th century, epigraphic documents passed to the public realm, as in the cippus of the Roman Forum, set in a place of worship dating from the first half of the 6th century BC, and covered in the mid-1st century BC with a new flooring in black marble (*Lapis Niger*). The inscription, the oldest on stone in Latin, contains the sacred law of the sanctuary, referring to judicial and political activities and a prescription for the king, who, with a herald, was to use a chariot. The *Lapis Satricanus* block was reused in the foundations of the sanctuary situated on the acropolis dedicated to *Mater Matuta*, the goddess of dawn, light and fertility, a base of a votive offering, erected by a group of *suodales*, companions, who, in the name of Mars, formed an armed company tied to *Poplios Valesios* perhaps *Publius Valerius Publicola*, first consul of the Republic together with *Lucius Giunius Brutus* in 509 BC.

From a tomb at Lanuvium comes the fine panoply (helmet and breastplate) of a warrior who combined his military role with a fond-

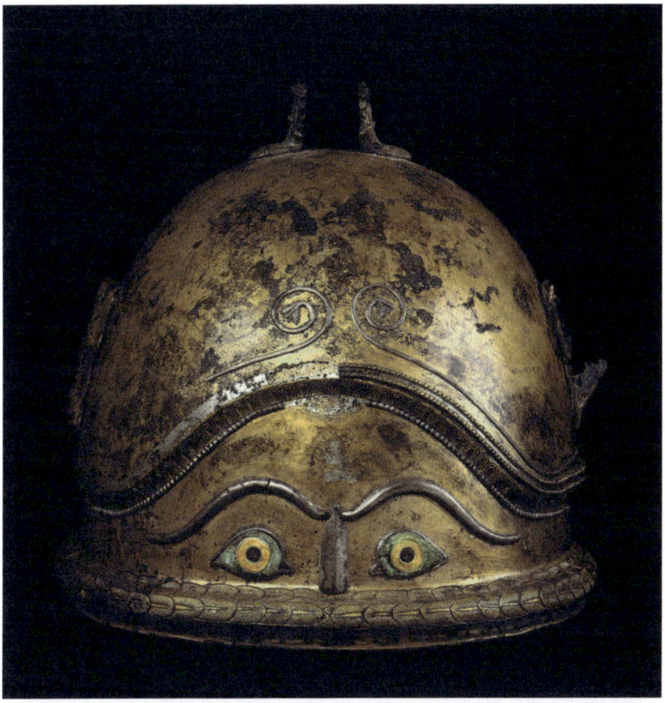

Helmet from the tomb of the warrior at Lanuvio.

Marble basin of fountain (*labrum*).

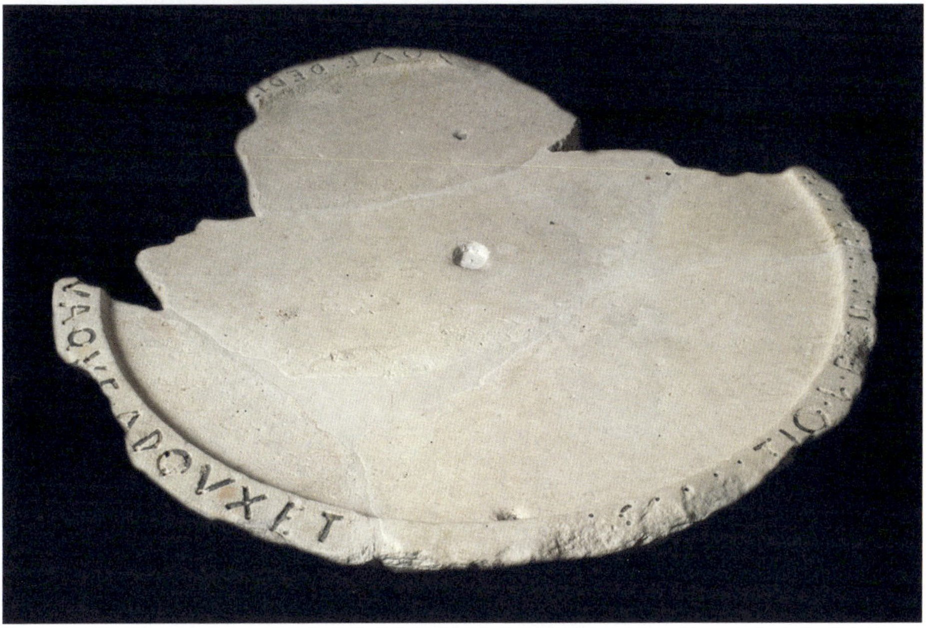

Beautiful Goddesses in Terracotta

In 1927 workers on a farm at the locality of Casaletto in Valle Ariccia brought to light the remains of a small sanctuary of considerable antiquity, whose votive deposit contained numerous figurative ex-votos, heads of men and women and anatomical offerings. In the sanctuary, an early phase oriented toward the sphere of *sanatio* or healing was followed at the end of the 4th century BC by a "refoundation" which had consequences on the architectural plane as well. To this phase belong the large clay sculptures, "Sicilian" in style, with the *megalai theai* represented in the form of busts, i.e. as they reemerge from the Underworld. The qualifying elements, such as the ears of grain interwoven with the hair or diadem, or the piglet that one of the seated figures held in her hand, point us in the direction of the religious world of Demeter and Kore. The half-length image is also employed to represent Demeter, even though it is specific to Kore/Persephone. In the latter case, in fact, the bust evokes the *anados*, the moment of return in her cyclic rise from the depths of the earth. Although data on the excavation are insufficient, we can imagine that there was a small *naos* inside the precinct, with a platform on which stood the divine busts, ascribable to more than one modeler in clay. An extremely refined sculptor must have been responsible for the more imposing and matronly bust of Demeter/Ceres, which depicts the goddess in majestic serenity and presents the happy ending to the mother's story and Zeus's eternal guarantee of the new order: nature has resumed its cycles of growth, the Great Goddesses protect the annual ripening of the crops and reveal to mortals the secrets of reproduction and the births of men and animals, ensuring the continuity of life. (N.G.)

Woman offering a piglet.

Bust of Demeter.

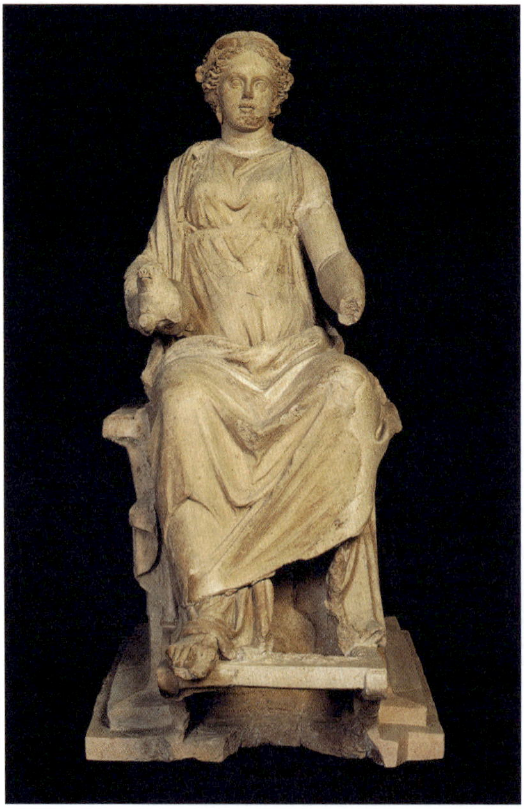

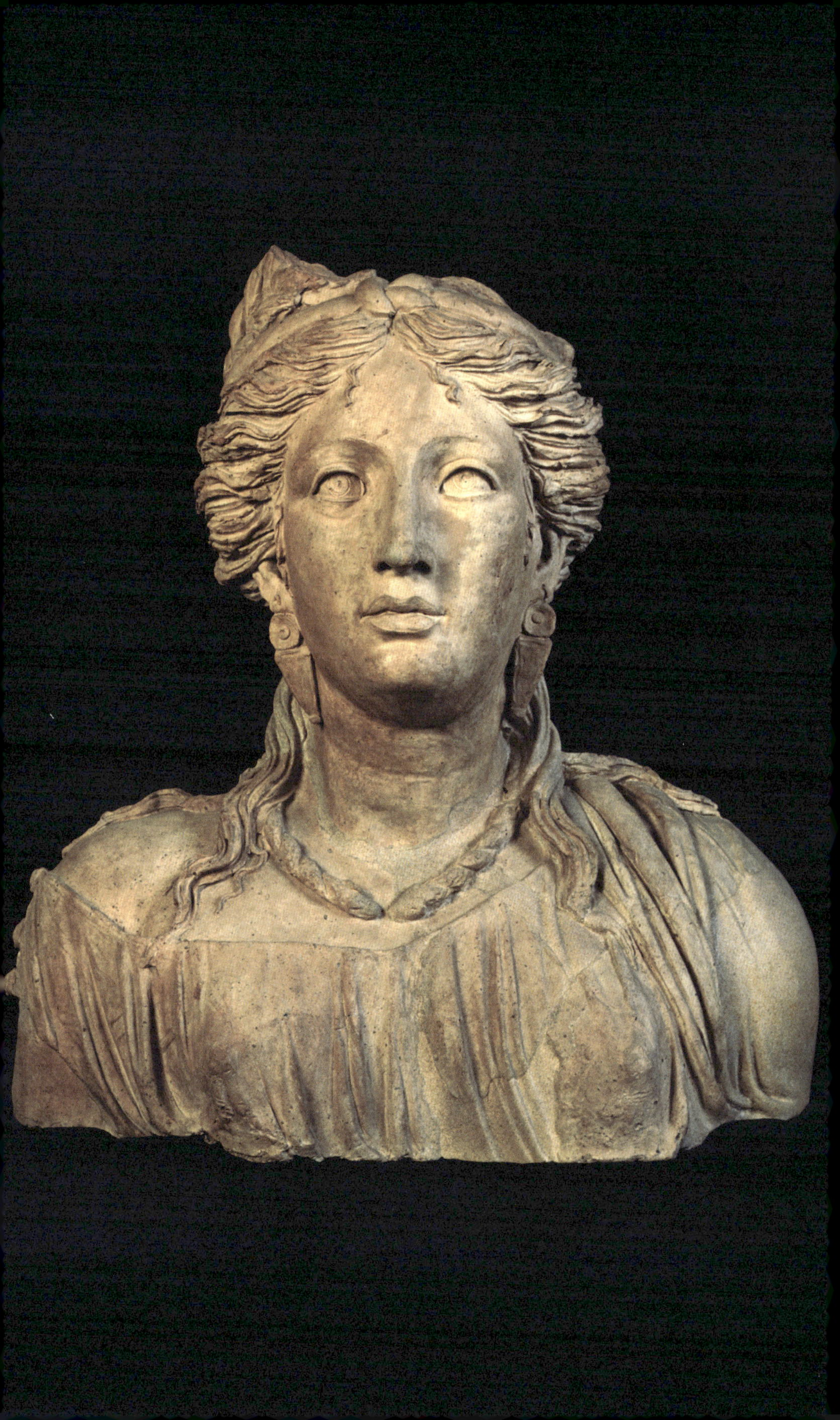

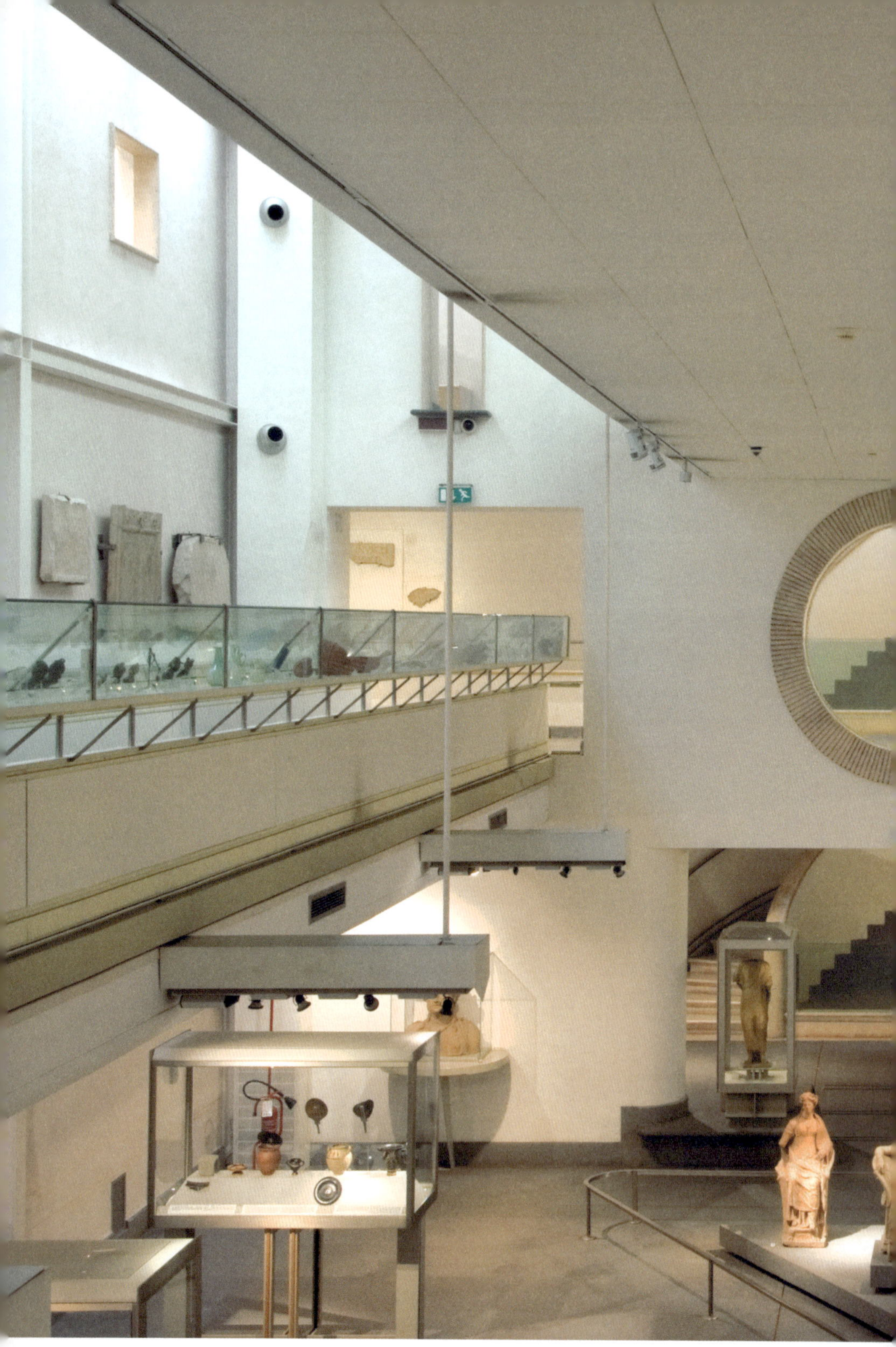

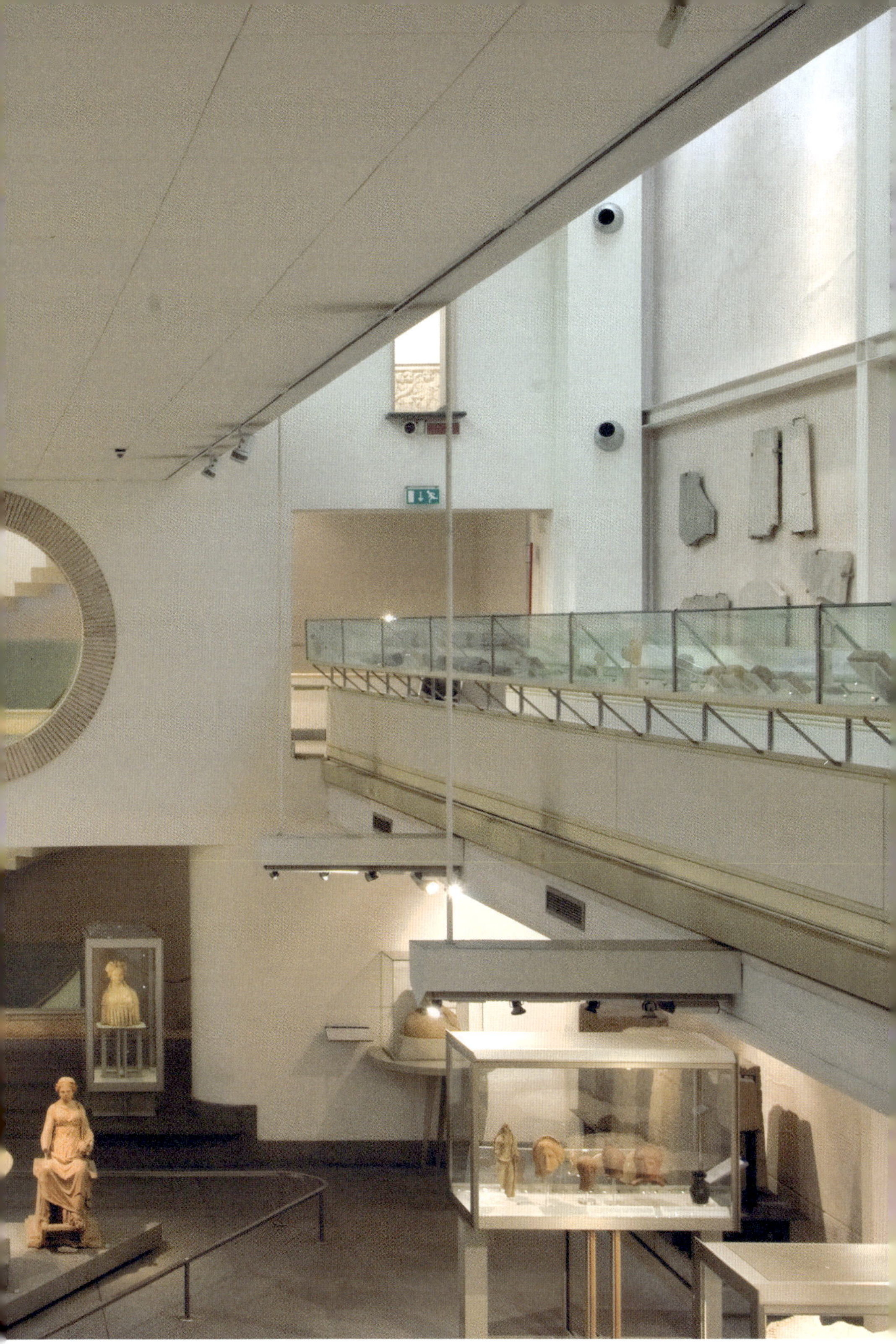

ness for the Greek culture of the gymnasium. This artefact is evidence of the intensity of contacts between Latium and the cities of *Magna Graecia* at the start of the 5th century BC.

Room III contains materials and inscriptions from the mid-Republican period (4th - 3rd centuries BC), coming from Rome and some other cities of Latium. In this period epigraphs were still fairly few in number, with a marked predominance of those of a sacred character, chiefly dedications and offerings that present a picture of the pantheon of gods worshipped at the time. Of particular interest is the small base of a donarium for Aesculapius from the temple on the Tiber Island; a limestone crown for the Fortuna Primigenia from the great sanctuary of Praeneste; and a peperino cippus offered to Aeneas, the Trojan hero venerated at the sanctuary of Lavinium as a Lar, i.e. a deified ancestor. From the sanctuary of Hercules at Borgo San Giovanni, near Lanuvium, comes a marble fountain basin (*labrum*) inscribed on the lip with a refined technique that involved the use of letters made of metal to compose the epigraph. The text, of an official nature, records the name of a local aedile who dedicated the monument. The room concludes with the exceptional votive complex of the sanctuary of Demeter and Kore at Aricia: dating from sometime between the late 4th century BC and the first half of the 3rd, it is made up of three seated statues and two terracotta busts of outstanding importance (see p. 18).

Previous pages
The hall of the Epigraphic Museum.

View of the second floor of the Epigraphic Museum.

Room IV is devoted to late-Republican inscriptions (2nd – 1st centuries BC). The achievement of Rome as ruler of a Mediterranean empire during the 2nd century BC is documented by the inscribed base of Lucius Mummius, consul in 146 BC, known above all for the destruction of the city of Corinth. Rome's new role also had repercussions on the political, social and economic structure, determining a series of changes that reached their climax in the 1st century BC. In the documents one finds the appearance of senators involved in political competitions – as in the bowls with inscriptions of electoral propaganda by Cato and Catiline – but especially a great number of freedmen who proudly displayed their status by creating their own burial places, simple inscribed cippi as well as reliefs with portraits. Even women, while still confined to a secondary social role, were able to attain a degree of independence from an economic and professional viewpoint, as demonstrated by the sepulchral inscription dedicated by *Gaavia Philumina*, who at her own expense erected a sepulchre for herself, her patron and another freedman. An exceptional testimony is that of the so-called *laudatio Turiae*, a funeral oration carved in marble for a courageous wife who had preserved the family estate at the time of the civil wars and also saved her husband's life.

Rooms V, VI, VII

A display of epigraphs from the Imperial period (1st – 4th centuries AD) begins in the last room on the ground floor. **Room V** illustrates the figure of the emperor and the role of inscriptions in the assertion and diffusion of the Imperial cult. Recent excavations on the north-eastern slopes of the Palatine Hill, near the Arch of Constantine, have revealed the area of the *Curiae Veteres*, an ancient sanctuary traditionally believed to be founded by Romulus. The architectural fragments from this area belong to a temple reconstructed after a fire by

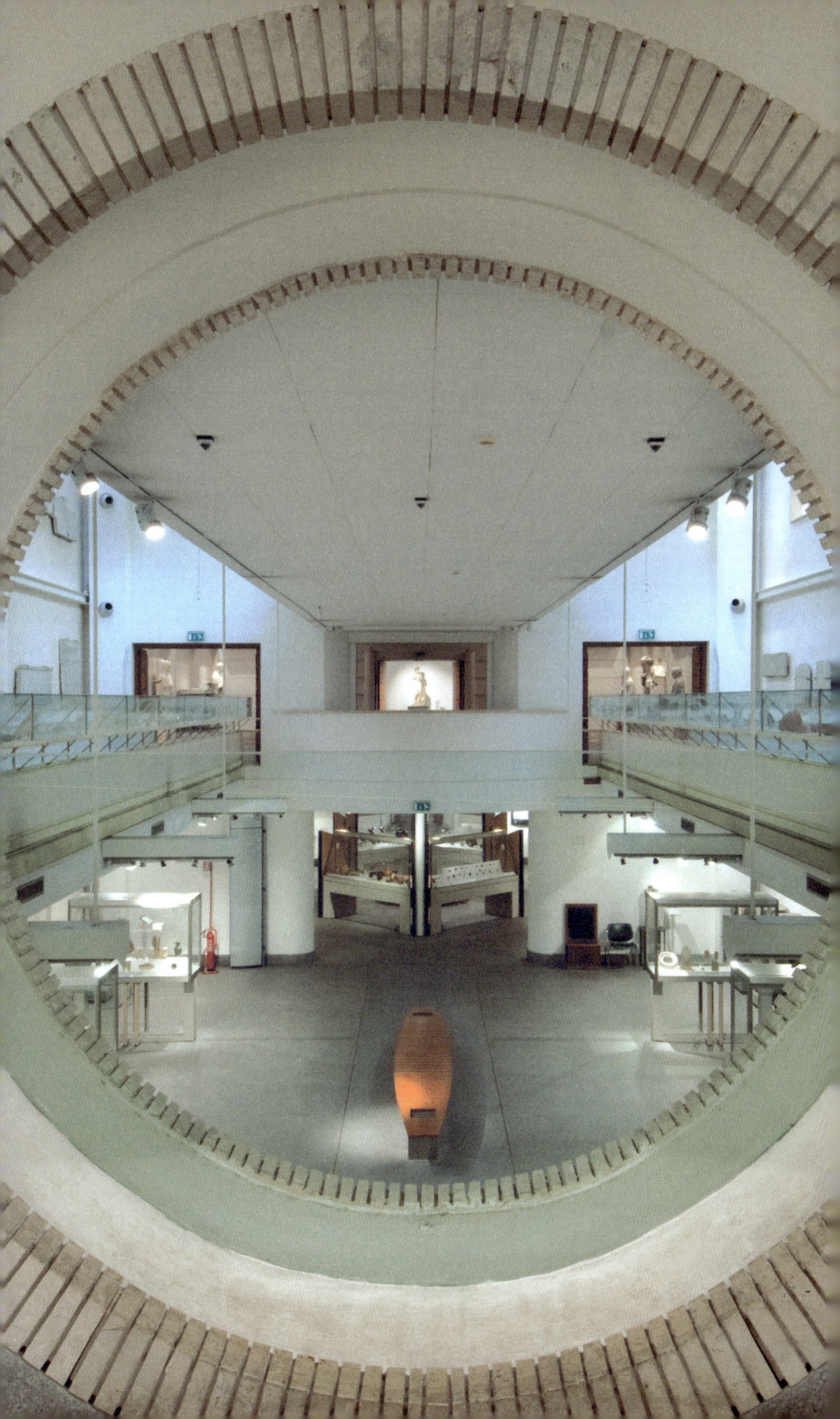

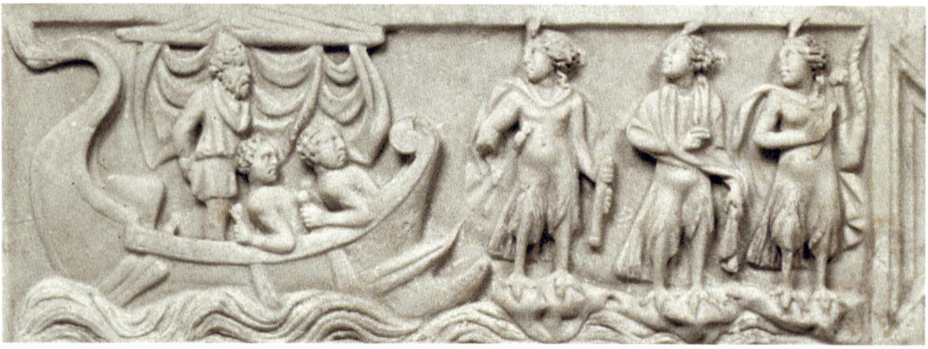

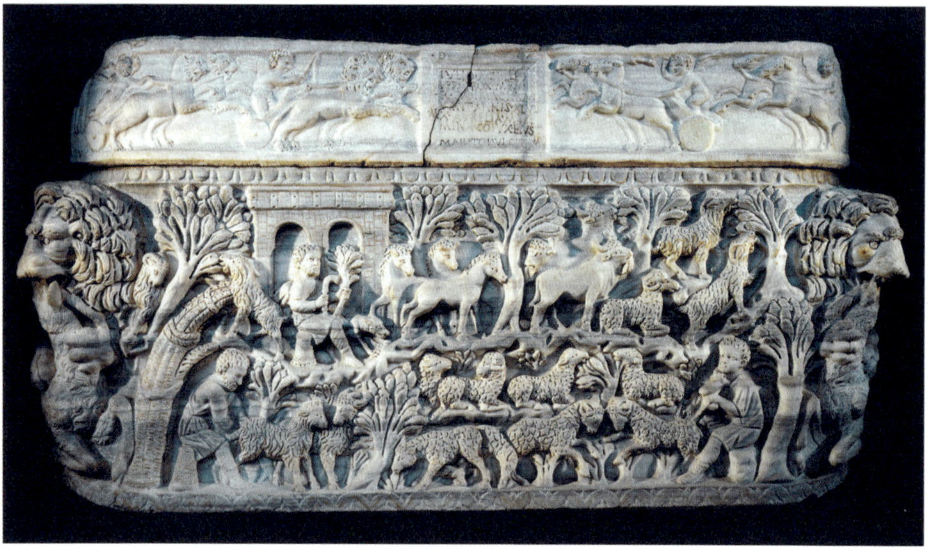

Ulysses and the Sirens, detail from the sarcophagus of the eques Marcus Aurelius Romanus.

Sarcophagus of Julius Achilleus with pastoral scenes.

Tabula alimentaria of the Ligures Baebiani, bronze.

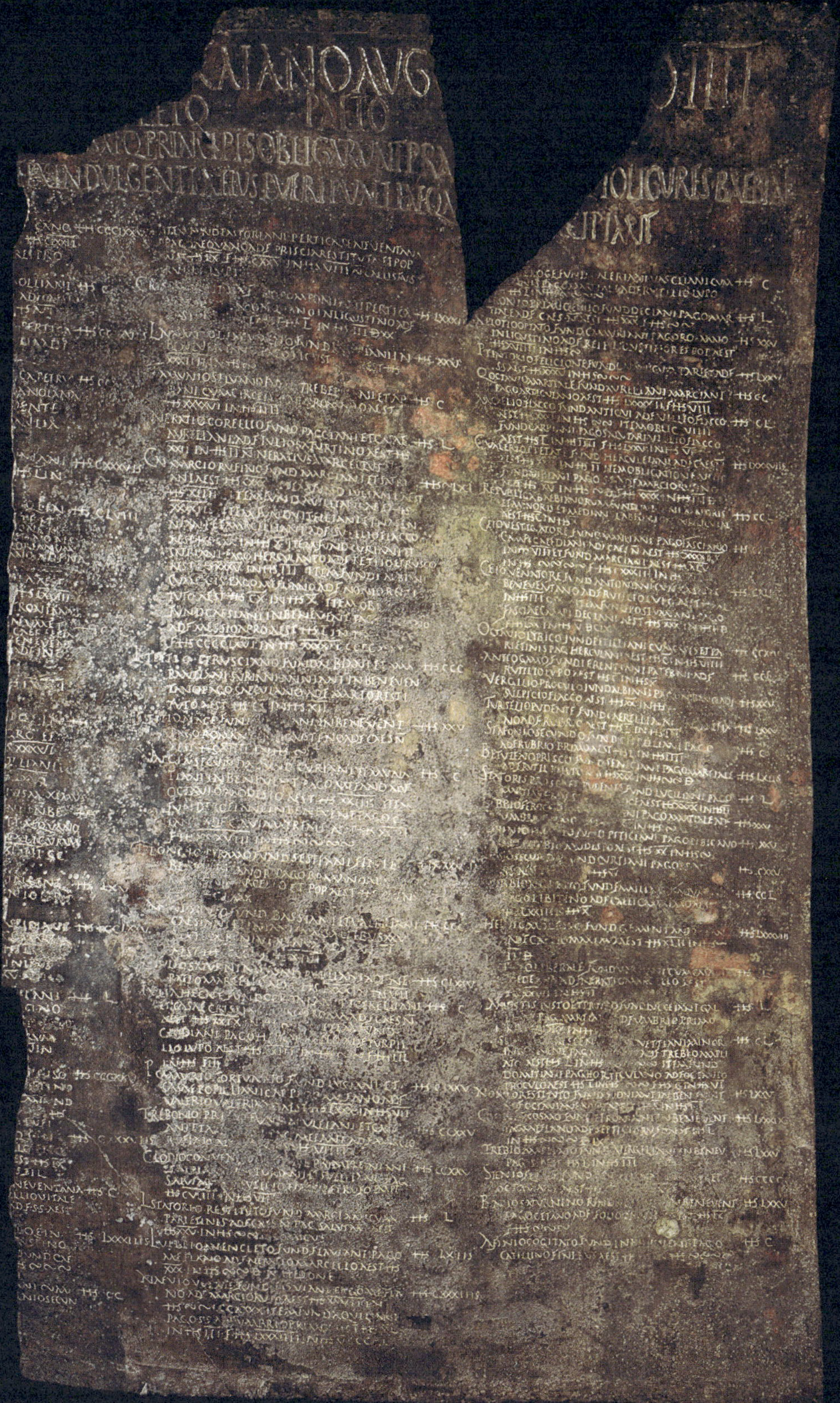
RAIANO AVG

the emperor Claudius at his own expense between 51 and 54 AD. It could be the main building of the *Curiae Veteres*, or the shrine consecrated to the memory of Augustus by his wife Livia. Near the temple, there was a monumental compound intended to honour Augustus and the members of his dynasty. The complex, created during the first Augustan period, went through many transformations and it was eventually destroyed by the great Neronian fire of 64 AD. The bronze base is dedicated to Tiberius, the marble one to Augustus, Claudius, Nero and Agrippina. The dedications were offered by the *aenatores*, the bronze wind instrument players who served in the solemn military and civic ceremonies: the *tubicines*, players of *tuba*, the *liticines*, players of *lituus*, and the *cornicines*, players of *cornu*. The room also contains two accounts of the cult of the Lares Compitales. Celebrated at crossroads (*compita*), the cult was intended to increase devotion to the emperor.

Room VI, laid out along the two walkways of the first floor, illustrates the structure of Roman society, presenting on the right the upper classes (the emperor with the imperial family and the senatorial order), and on the left the middle classes, including the military, the artisans responsible for large-scale production, the class of powerful freedmen and imperial slaves. The exhibits include numerous fragments of *fistulae*, the lead pipes used to connect the aqueducts to public buildings or residences belonging to members of the highest classes. The same social classes were frequently proprietors of large factories producing building materials, documented by the numerous fragments of bricks with kiln marks. The central space between the two walkways is dedicated to the equestrian class and the *apparitores*, i.e. the magistrates' assistants. The large sarcophagus with pastoral scenes was intended for *Iulius Achilleus*, a high-ranking official of the equestrian class who, after being responsible for the archives of the imperial chancellery, served as superintendent of the *Ludus Magnus*, the barracks of gladiators situated near the Colosseum. In reference to the category of *apparitores*, meanwhile, one finds a cinerary altar of the scribes, intended for two brothers who were both in the service of the curule aediles with financial and administrative posts, and a relief with the *fasces* as a symbol of the lectors who used them to guard the principal magistrates.

Room VII displays epigraphs related to the politico-administrative institutions, presenting the main senatorial posts and those of the equestrian order. Of particular interest is the fragment of the funerary inscription of the historian Tacitus; although few letters are preserved, it is possible to recognise some positions of his career. The bronze portrait of L. Cornelius Pusio is also remarkable; the head belonged to a statue placed on a base of which the inscription, commemorating his career, was the front cover. The traditional posts of the *cursus honorum* established in the Republican period were joined by others in the Imperial period, such as the *praefectura urbis*, with policing and judiciary power, and the *praefectura Alimentorum* which is referenced in the bronze *tabula alimentaria* from the city of the *Ligures Baebiani*, near Benevento. The slab contains a list of repayable loans granted to landowners and secured by mortgages on land value; the capital resulting from such interest

was destined for the maintenance of the children of poor families in the area so according to the measure instituted by Trajan with the name *insitutio alimentaria*.
Other prefectures represented the apex of the equestrian career, however: that of the *annona*, documented in the slab of G. Junius Flavianus, which ensured Rome's food supply, while the responsibilities of that of the *praetorium* included command of the emperor's armed guard. The career of Commodus's praetorian prefect, *Lucius Iulius Vehilius Iulianus*, is exceptional; in spite of the important military commands alternating with administrative tasks of progressively higher rank, the emperor Commodus killed him after many humiliations inflicted.

Rooms VIII, IX, X

In **Room VIII** we find documents relating to economic activities, throwing light on various aspects of commerce, production and handicrafts in the Roman world. The first inscriptions concern the management and administration of the *horrea*, the great warehouses that were used to store foodstuffs, thereby guaranteeing the capital's food supply (the *annona*). One that stands out is the funerary altar of Aurelia Nais, a *piscatrix* (fish vendor) who worked in Rome's largest complex of food warehouses located in the present-day Testaccio area. A great deal of space is also devoted to single trades and crafts, both through presentation of the "guilds" (*collegia*), such as the *collegium thurariorum et unguentariorum* (unguent and incense vendors) or the *calcarienses* (sellers of lime), and also individually as in the case of *Sellia Epyre*, who made and sold garments decorated with gold (*auri vestrix*), or *M. Antonius Teres*, a livestock merchant (*negotiator suariae et pecuariae*). There are also professional performers such as the renowned pantomime *L. Aurelius Apolaustus Memphius*, who won numerous theatrical competitions and was accepted among the decurions of Tivoli; the comical actor (*comoedus*) *P. Vinicius Laces*; and some reliefs that commemorate gladiators' performances. Evidence of slavery's role in the economy of the Roman world is provided by a bronze collar belonging to a slave. In the event of the slave's escape, the text promised a reward to whoever returned him to his owner Zonino.

With **Room IX** we enter the world of Roman religion, characterised by a great variety of cults. Alongside public religion, which was the domain of institutions that acted on behalf of the Roman people,

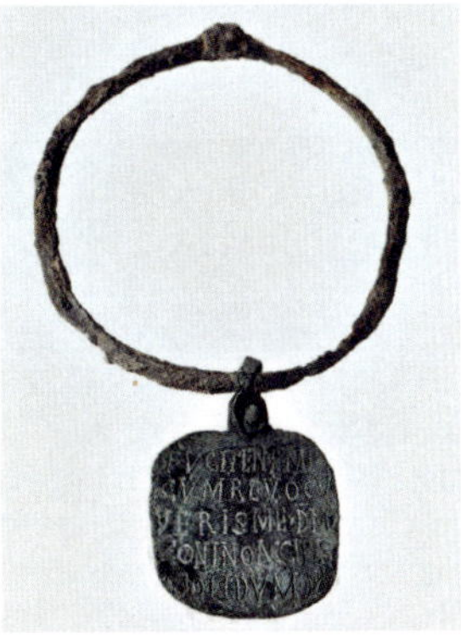

Iron collar of a slave.

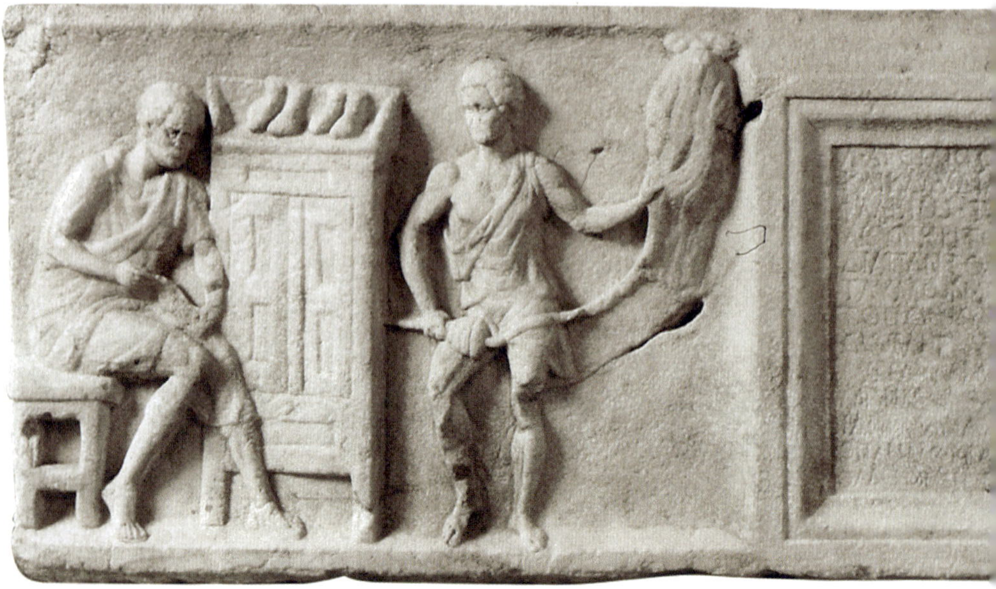

Front of the sarcophagus of *Titus Flavius Trophimas* with scenes of craftsmen at work.

there were also domestic rituals such as those attested to by dedications to the Penates, the Lares and the personal *Genius*. The sepulchres were instead entrusted to the Manes, the collective of the divinised souls of the dead, who were to guarantee the sepulchres' sacredness. The dedication to these divinities became part of the formulary of sepulchral inscriptions, and was even maintained among the accounts of Christians (as in the stele of *Licinia Amias*). The divinities also sometimes appeared on funerary steles, as with the sepulchral inscription of the young *Sextius Rufus Achilleus*, who died when he was just seven months old and is portrayed as Mercury the psychopomp, a divinity accompanying deceased souls to the afterlife. Between the late 2nd and early 3rd centuries, one also starts to see the diffusion of inscriptions by the first Christians. Prevalently of a funerary nature, these inscriptions adopted unique symbols such as the fish (using the Greek term *ichthys*, meaning fish, as an acronym of the words "Jesus Christ, Son of God, our Saviour"), the anchor, the dove or the characteristic expressions *in pace* or *in Christ* (see the slab of *Priscus*). In Rome there was also a thriving Jewish community, as demonstrated by the sarcophagus cover of Faustina, on which the usual decoration of theatrical masks is flanked by Hebrew symbols of the *Menorah*, or seven-branched lampstand, the *shofar*, or ritual horn, the *lulav*, or palm branch, and the Hebrew term *shalom*, meaning peace.

Eastern religions were also widely diffused, particularly the cults of Isis, Mithras, Sol, Sabazios, Jupiter Heliopolitanus and Jupiter Dolichenus. The statue of Isis, dating from the late 2nd century AD and the early 3rd century AD, represents the goddess wearing the *basileion*, the headgear with the sun disk, the crescent and the horns of a cow, while the altar dedicated to her priestess *Cantinea Procla* is decorated with the symbols of her role (the *basileion* formed

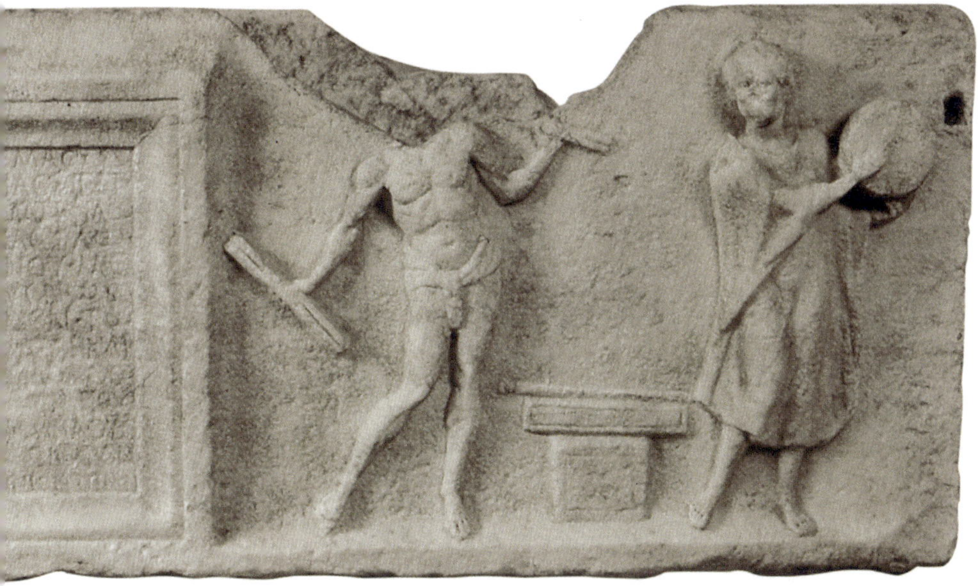

by two ears of wheat surmounted by a snake, the fringed cloak and the pitcher). Many of the inscriptions concern the worship of the god Mithras, usually depicted in the act of the *tauroctonia*, the ritual killing of the bull, as it appears in the polychrome relief from the Mithraeum of Santo Stefano Rotondo, where the small statue portraying the god emerging from the rock, *petrogenitus*, was also found. The large relief of Mithras Tauroctonos has been recently reconstructed in its entirety thanks to a collaborative agreement with the Badisches Landesmuseum in Karlsruhe. It was found in 1964 at Tor Cervara during work to remove wartime debris which probably broke the relief into many fragments. The fragment depicting the face of Mithras had ended up in the Karlsruhe Museum, where it was identified as belonging to this relief and has now been returned to its original position.

Room X is dedicated to magic in the Roman world. The votive hand *pantea* (*Hand*-of-the-All-Goddess) in the position of divine benediction and covered with animals and symbols, together with the magic nail, with an invocation to Iao (Iahveh) Sabaoth and a series of symbols and animals in a composite scheme referring to the evil eye, are both associated with the cult of Sabatius. Small amulets were also worn with a salutary and protective function, such as the silver *tempietto* ("small temple") inscribed with biblical quotes, and little objects that referred to the sexual sphere (the small *phallus*, the male sexual organ, or the *manus obscaena*, a fist with a clenched thumb). There are also several *defixiones* with a variety of origins. These thin sheets of lead were often pierced with nails and are inscribed with magic symbols and curses against charioteers, horses and a hated woman. The material originating from the recent discovery of the fountain of Anna Perenna is also remarkable (see p. 33). (C.C.-M-C.)

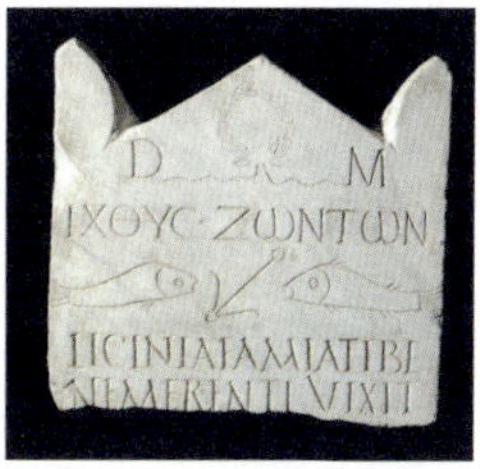

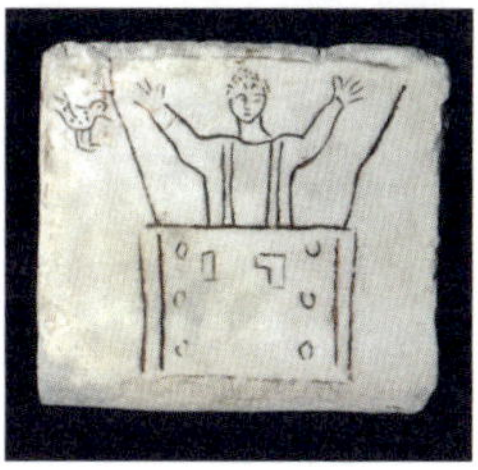

Funerary stele of *Licinia Amias*.

Slab carved with the scene of Noah on the Ark, taken from the book of Genesis.

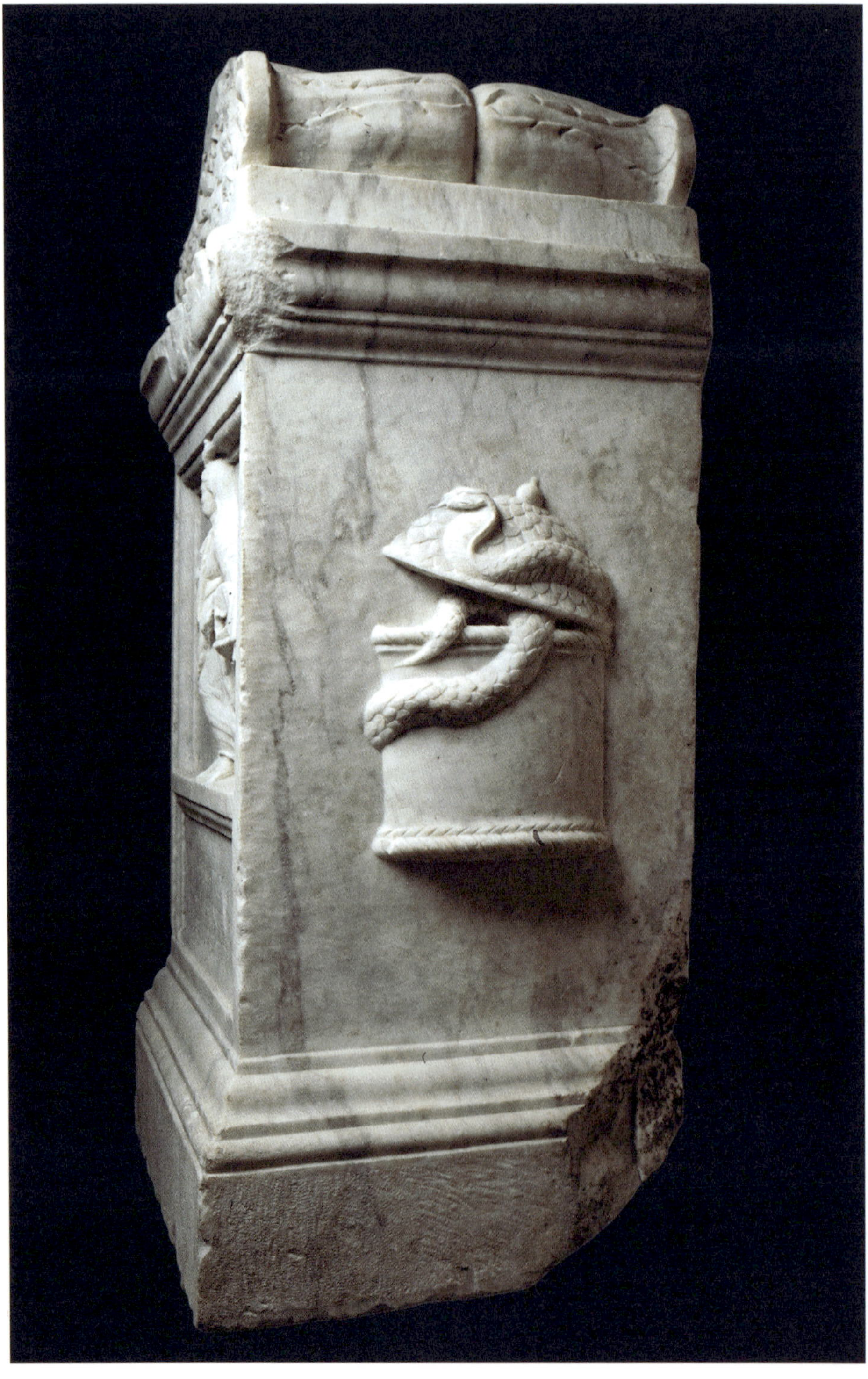

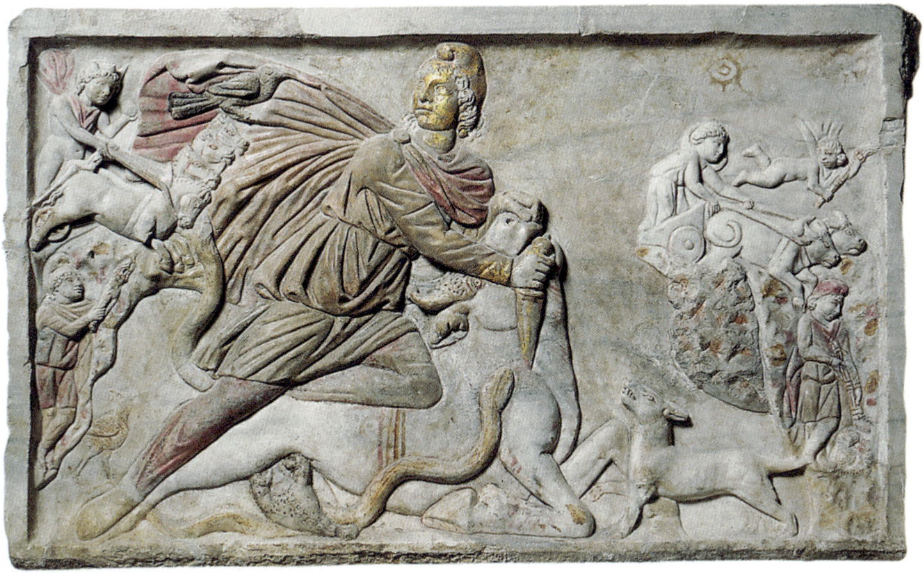

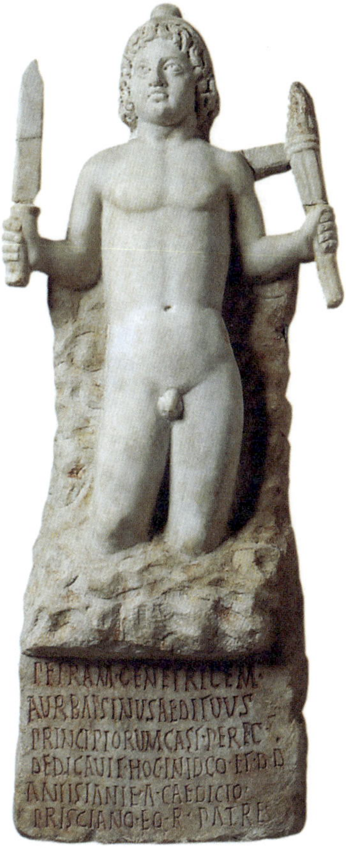

Funerary altar
of *Cantinea Procla*.

Relief with Mithras
Tauroctonus from Santo
Stefano Rotondo.

Mithras Petrogenitus.

The Eulogy of *Allia Potestas*

Funerary inscriptions often provide information about the life of the deceased, usually in a formal manner but sometimes telling the story of individuals in a more “familiar” way. In 1912 an elegant slab of marble was discovered in the Salario burial ground, near the Via Pinciana, that must have been attached with nails and has been dated to the first half of the 2nd century AD on linguistic grounds. Care was taken over the layout of the text.
The customary formula of dedication to the Manes, *Dis Manib(us)*, is inscribed at the top in larger letters and beneath it is set the name of the deceased, Allia Potestas, freedwoman of Allius. In the two columns underneath are carved the poetic text of her funeral *elogium*, written in hexameters and all of fifty lines long. The last two lines contain an invitation not to profane the grave.
The poem is written in a style influenced by Ovid, although its author cannot have been very adept, as he uses a frequently colloquial and occasionally naïve language and sometimes forgets to respect the meter. It is likely that he was Allius, Allia’s patron, who speaks in the first person in the poem.
In any case he has followed, albeit in his own way, the tradition of the *laudatio funebris*, which was normally split into three parts: the lament over the death, an illustration of the deceased’s merits and a description of the grief of those who remain. The first lines, after the unusual reference to the woman’s birth at Perugia, contain concepts commonly found in epitaphs: the idea that a small urn is able to contain the body of such a grand woman and the complaint that Persephone and Fate always take the best things away. The description of Allia’s qualities is much more original, because in addition to the customary moral virtues (those normally ascribed to the matron) and practical merits, such as skill in weaving, industriousness or an abstinence from gossip, it dwells on her physical traits. Both the length and the wording used are out of the ordinary and suggest an intimate knowledge of the woman on the author’s part: he praises her shining eyes, blond hair, breasts, ivory skin and legs, which remind him of those of Atalanta (the swift-footed huntress) in theatrical performances. Perhaps her only defect was her rough hands.
The following lines are somewhat enigmatic and praise Allia for having been able to maintain harmony between two young lovers, who behaved like Orestes and Pylades (a celebrated pair of friends in mythology), living peacefully together in the same house as long as Allia was alive, only to grow old separately after her death. It is likely that Allia was the concubine of her grieving patron, while it is not clear who the two young men were, the patron himself and a friend or two other men. In any case the inscription records and commends the woman’s polyandry in a surprising way.
The final part of the text is reserved for the grief of the inconsolable patron, who now awaits his own death, wearing a gold bracelet inscribed with Allia’s name and adoring her image, which he wants to place in his tomb. The man also asserts that the woman is destined to live forever in his verses and concludes with another expression of pain at his loss. (M.C.)

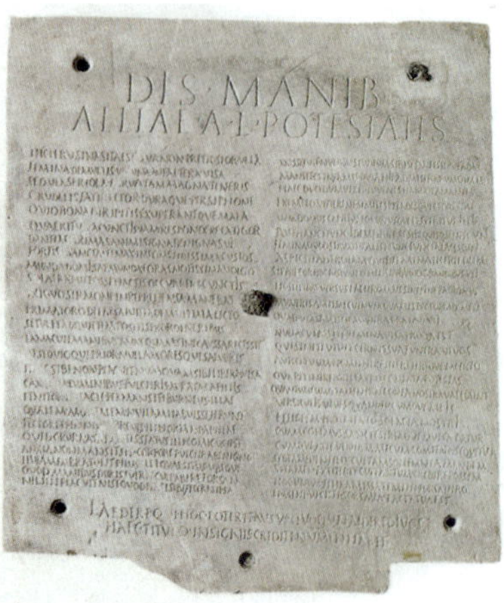

The eulogy of *Allia Potestas*.

The Fountain of Anna Perenna

The Fountain of Anna Perenna was discovered in 1999 during work to construct an underground parking facility in Piazza Euclide in Parioli. It is undoubtedly one of the most important discoveries relating to magic ever made, due to the richness and variety of material found in this single context. The fountain was a *krene*, functioning by direct uptake of rising spring-water. It had a very long life, from the 4th century BC to the 5th century AD.
Inside the cistern were found artefacts relating to religious practices, such as the 523 coins thrown into the water for good luck, pine cones and eggs as symbols of fertility, and even 75 lamps, some of them votive offerings. There were also found diverse and unusual magical artefacts; a large copper pot used for witches' magical potions, and several new lamps made of purified clay probably for spells, as described in the Hellenistic-period manual of magic, the Greek Magical Papyri. Six of the lamps have curses (*defixiones*) inscribed inside them. In total, 23 *defixiones* have been found inside the cistern, a significant discovery in a single context. Rarer still are the 24 lead containers stacked one inside the other, within them seven figurines made of some organic material. These must have been used to make spells and perform magical rituals against enemies or lovers. The amount of magical material concentrated in such a small space suggests that the fountain was a place well-known for finding magical practitioners. Among the many eastern deities invoked in the curses is Christ, who was considered a great healer and magician.
Anna was an ancient nymph whose cult centre was on the Via Flamina. On 15th March a wild festival took place to celebrate her cult, described in detail by Ovid in the *Fasti*. The place where it was found has been preserved and can be visited. An altar and two inscribed dedicatory bases, dating to the 2nd century AD, were built into the structure of the fountain during its final restoration. The altar was dedicated by Suetonius Germanus and his wife Licinia in fulfilment of a vow to Anna Perenna for a victory. This alludes to victory in a contest during the Ides of March celebrations, perhaps a competition to drink the most cups of wine or singing or mime contests. (M.P.)

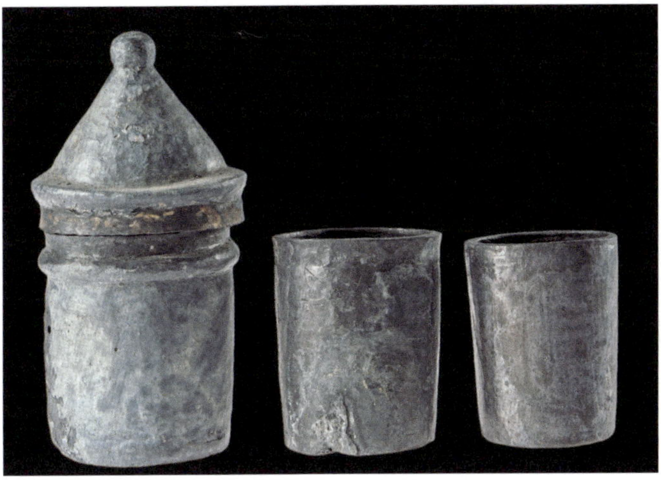

Inscribed magic container composed of three cylindrical vases inserted into each other.

An Idol for a Secret Ritual

At the beginning of the 20th century the remains of a small shrine dedicated to Syrian deities were found on the southeastern side of the Janiculum: Baal, venerated in Rome as Jupiter Heliopolitanus, and the minor divinities of the Heliopolitan triad: Atargatis (whom the Romans called Syrian Venus) and Simios (Mercury).

It is the last phase of the shrine, dating from the mid-4th century AD, that has been uncovered, and its plan reflects precise ritual requirements. Around a large courtyard, where the worshipers probably gathered, are set two groups of structures: to the west a building with a basilican plan, used for daily rites as is apparent from the marble statue of the god (perhaps Jupiter Heliopolitanus), found in the niche at the rear, and to the east a room with a mixtilinear plan. At the center of the latter stood a triangular altar with a hollow that housed the famous bronze idol, still covered with votive offerings (eggs, flowers, seeds) at the time of its discovery. The small idol represents a male figure, wrapped by seven coils of a snake that allude to the seven celestial spheres, and has been identified as the Egyptian Osiris or the Syrian Adonis, gods who were born and died each year and were both linked with the cycle of the seasons. In order to act out the allegory of the death and rebirth of the god, and therefore of the neophyte before and after initiation, the statuette was periodically taken out of its hiding place, venerated by the priests and worshipers and then put back again until the next ceremony of initiation into the mystery cult. (N.G.)

Two photographs taken at the moment of discovery of the altar containing the bronze idol during the excavation carried out by Paul Gauckler (1908-1910). Rome, Via Dandolo, Syrian sanctuary.

The idol in the pit photographed at the moment of its discovery.

Front and back of the Janiculum idol.

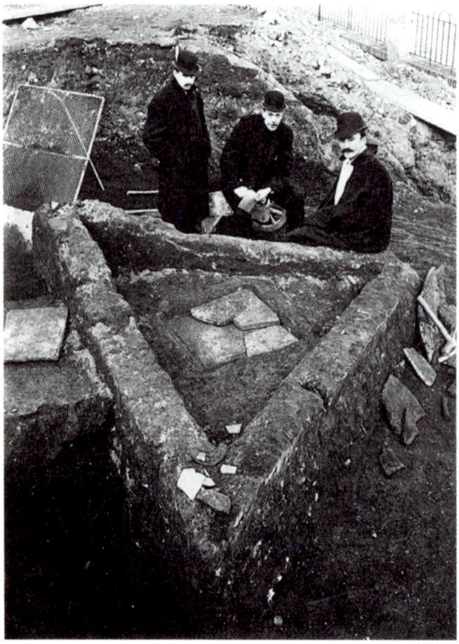

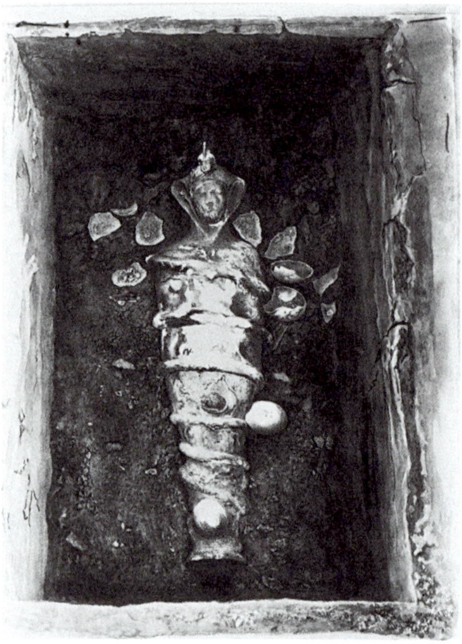

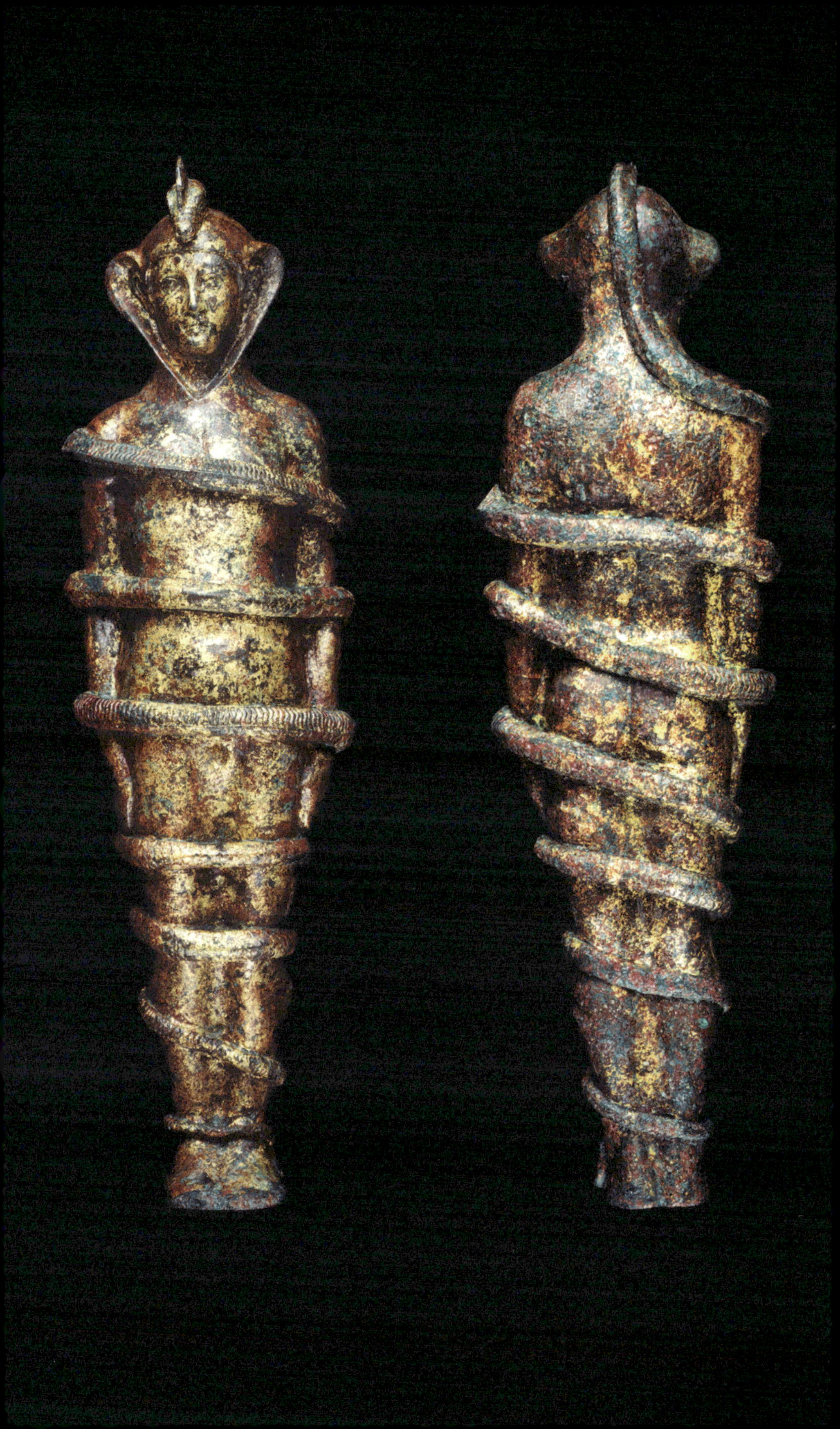

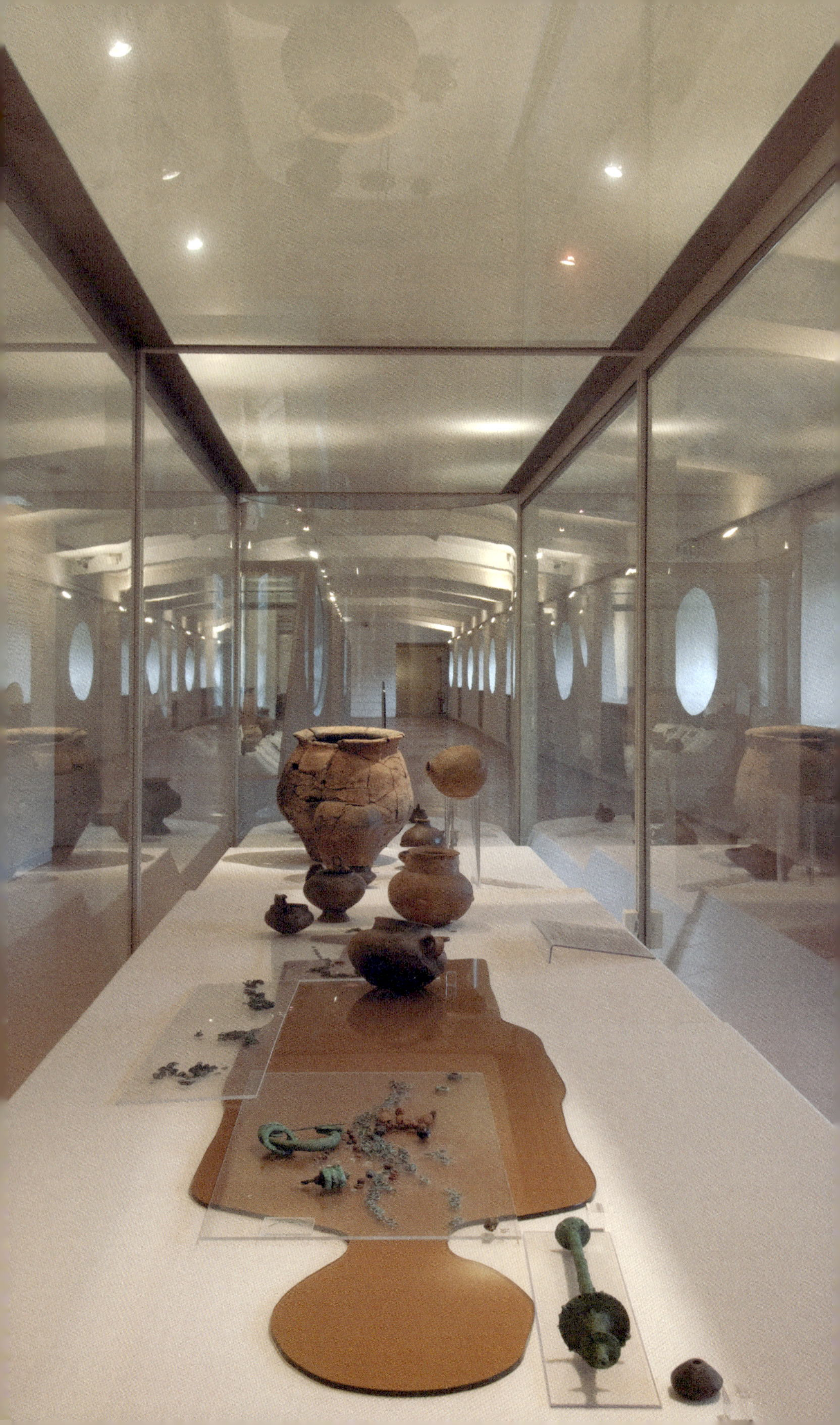

The Proto-History Museum

This section of the National Roman Museum, hosted on the first floor of Michelangelo's cloister and directly accessible from hall X of the Epigraphic Museum, illustrates the development of Latial culture from the late Bronze Age (11th century BC) and Iron Age up to the Orientalising period (10th – early 6th centuries BC), through the archaeological complexes that have been systematically explored and excavated in the area around Rome. The underlying prospect of the exhibition criteria is to use archaeology as a direct means of ethnographic and historical reconstruction, with an anthropological approach to the materials and contexts.
The first part of the exhibit has a general character and concerns all of ancient Latium (the territory stretching from the Tiber to Mount

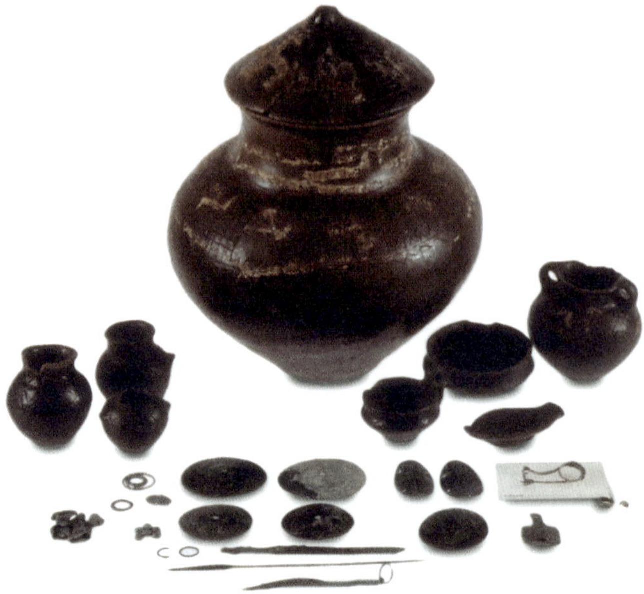

Page 36
A view of the proto-historic section of the museum.

Contents of the male cremation tomb in Pit 1, Quadrato (Rome) (Latial Period I).

Circeo) within the setting of the peninsula's Tyrrhenian regions. The archaeological materials serve to reconstruct the social structure, economy, religion, ideology, territorial and political organisation, relations with neighbouring regions and long-distance connections.
The period of time examined witnessed a profound transformation of Latium's communities. This change was partly driven by contacts with nearby regions: Etruria to the north, where the politico-territorial system of large Villanovan proto-cities developed, and Campania to the south, where the earliest Greek colonisation took root during the 8th century BC. The illustration of the overall characteristics and development of Latial culture is followed by examples of individual towns in the vicinity of Rome.

Latial Culture

This general section provides information on the geographic and historical context within which the prehistory and proto-history of Latium developed. The section illustrates the sequence of pre-history and proto-history in Latium, from the Lower Palaeolithic to the Iron Age, along with the region's geological and territorial context. For the period corresponding to the development of Latial culture, between the late Bronze Age and the early Iron Age (11th – 10th centuries BC), the data originating from the Gabii-Castiglione area allows a reconstruction of the natural and man-made environment. Investigations in the region's necropolises and built-up areas, meanwhile, offer data on the primary economy, demography, settlement and the development of the social structure and political organisation over time. Regarding the earliest periods, the archaeological data and information from the sources all highlight the central role of the Alban Hills as a point of reference for the entire region. As of Latial Period IIB (10th – 9th centuries BC), the development of connections with Etruria and Campania – via the Tiber and

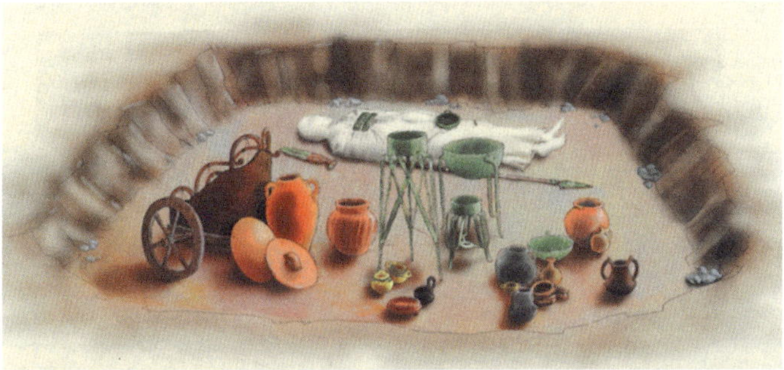

Graphic reconstruction of tomb 15 at Castel di Decima, a pit containing a male interment (Latial period IVa).

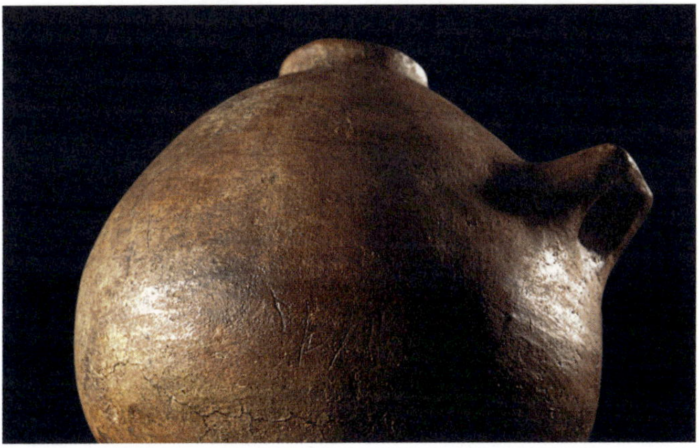

Flask with Greek inscription from tomb 482 in the necropolis of Osteria dell'Osa.

the Valle Latina – determined a loss of importance for the Alban Hills and an increase in the role of Rome. In the period between the 11th and early 6th centuries BC, Latium's communities evolved from egalitarian tribal structures, organised in village communities, to complex socio-political structures based on nobility and patronage, organised in proto-urban and subsequently urban forms. The tombs' burial artefacts reflect the changes that occurred within the communities. The closing phase of the final Bronze Age (11th – 10th centuries BC, Latial Period I) corresponds to the emergence of a specific cultural aspect of ancient Latium. The small groups of cremation tombs with miniaturised grave goods of this period reveal the figures of chiefs who were invested with political and religious power, often brought together in the same person (as can be observed in Tomb 1 at Quadrato di Torre Spaccata exhibited in the museum). These chiefs were responsible for guiding the region's process of cultural and political transformation.

In Latial Period II (circa 10th – 9th centuries BC, early Iron Age), Latium's process of socio-political structuring developed further. The funeral ritual was extended to the entire community; burial appeared alongside cremation and subsequently became the predominant ritual. In the necropolis, the spatial distribution of tombs in groups (probably of kinship) together with the grave goods reproduce the community's organisation and the roles played by its members during their lives. Starting in Latial Period III (late 9th – 8th centuries BC), the tombs' arrangement on the

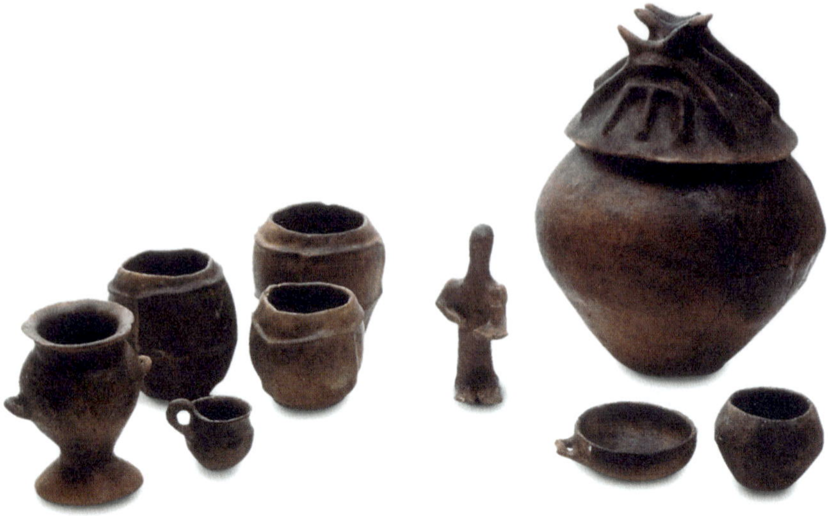

ground of the necropolis and the composition of burial artefacts document the emergence of an aristocratic-type ideology. The process of division into social classes reached completion by Latial Period IV (late 8th – early 6th centuries BC). The princely tombs, which characterise the earliest stage of this period, reveal the climax in the structuring of the aristocracies. Around the mid-7th century BC, the ruling stratum of society, which was now distinguished by the adoption of chamber tombs containing multiple entombments, no longer sacrificed great riches in their burial places, but directed their economic investments towards the development of towns and the territory.

In the four centuries that witnessed the unfolding of Latial culture, artisan production underwent a widespread transformation that led to an increase in output, the professional specialisation of craftsmen, and the standardisation of forms and types.

Over time, inter-regional connections also varied in intensity and direction. In Latial Period I, *Latium vetus* displayed very strong links with southern Etruria, evidenced by the great similarity in cremation rituals featuring miniaturised tomb goods, as well as in certain types of bronzes. In Latial Period II, the strongest and most systematic connections were instead with coeval communities in Campania and Calabria. One of the most remarkable documents attesting to Latium's intense connections

Contents of the male cremation Tomb in Pit 142, necropolis of Osteria dell'Osa (Latial Period II).

Grave goods of Tomb 32, containing the interment of a child in the necropolis of Castiglione (Latial Period II).

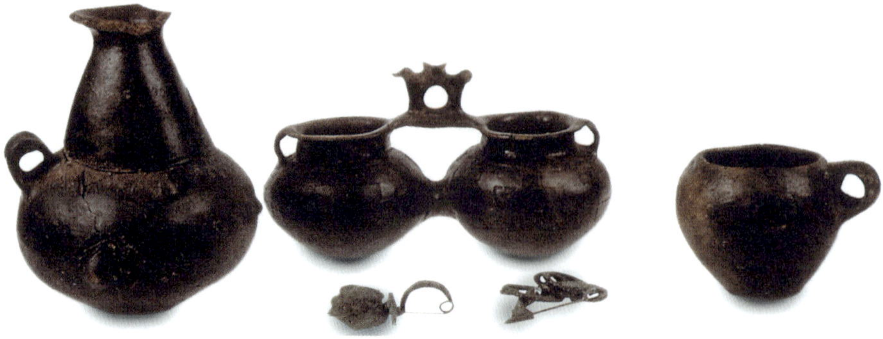

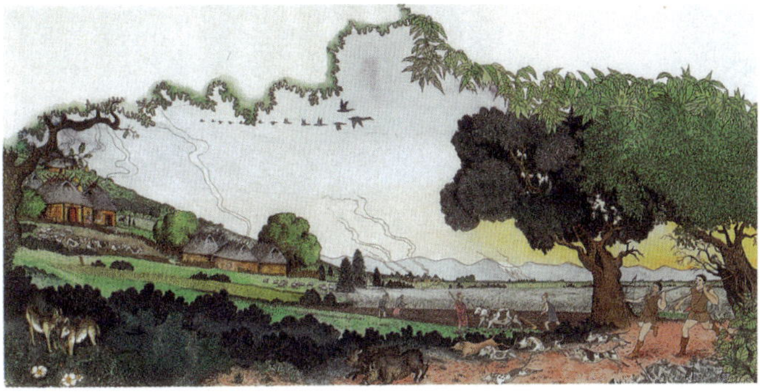

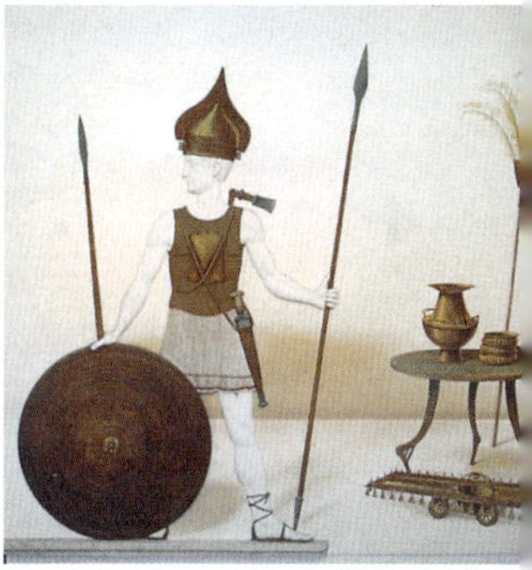

Reconstruction of the contents of a warrior's tomb (Tomb 600) in the necropolis of Osteria dell'Osa (Latial Period III).

Reconstruction of the setting of the krater at Castiglione.

with south Tyrrhenian regions is the vase with an inscription in Greek letters from Tomb 482 at the necropolis of Osteria dell'Osa, dating from Period IIB (9th century BC), exhibited in the section dedicated to this necropolis. With the start of Latial Period III, the strongest and most systematic contacts shifted from southern Italy to Villanovan Etruria. As a result, Rome assumed a fundamental role not only as an obligatory point of passage between Latium and Etruria, but also as an intermediary for connections between Etruria and Campania – links which became particularly important with the onset of Greek colonisation. In the subsequent Orientalising period, Latium, like most regions in the Mediterranean basin, was struck by a substantial influx of prestigious and luxury objects originating from Greece and the East, brought above all by Phoenician merchants.

Major Towns

This section exhibits the archaeological complexes, in particular built-up areas and necropolises, discovered in the area around Rome, each of which has its own characteristics requiring a specific space. The section includes the two necropolises of the Gabii area (the future Latin city on the Via Praenestina), or rather the burial grounds of Osteria dell'Osa and Castiglione. At the centre of the area lies the ancient volcanic crater of Castiglione, which in historical times was occupied by a lake. In the early Iron Age (10th – 8th centuries BC), the edge and part of the zone inside the crater hosted a series of small settlements with their necropolises. The Osteria dell'Osa burial ground probably belonged to one of the most important villages, while the Castiglione site belonged to a smaller and shorter-lived settlement. In the second half of the 8th century BC, inhabitants of villages scattered around the area were concentrated on the crater's southeast edge, initiating a process that led to the founding of the Latin city of Gabii at the end of the 7th century BC.
The necropolis of Osteria dell'Osa provides the most extensive and comprehensive documentation for Period II of Latial culture (10th – 9th centuries BC). The tombs (numbering about 450) are divided into groups that correspond to the extended families that formed the community. The grave goods show a clear division of horizontal and vertical roles according to sex and age group. In a large showcase in the museum's first room dedicated to Osteria dell'Osa, the spatial distribution has been reconstructed along with characteristics of the burial places belonging

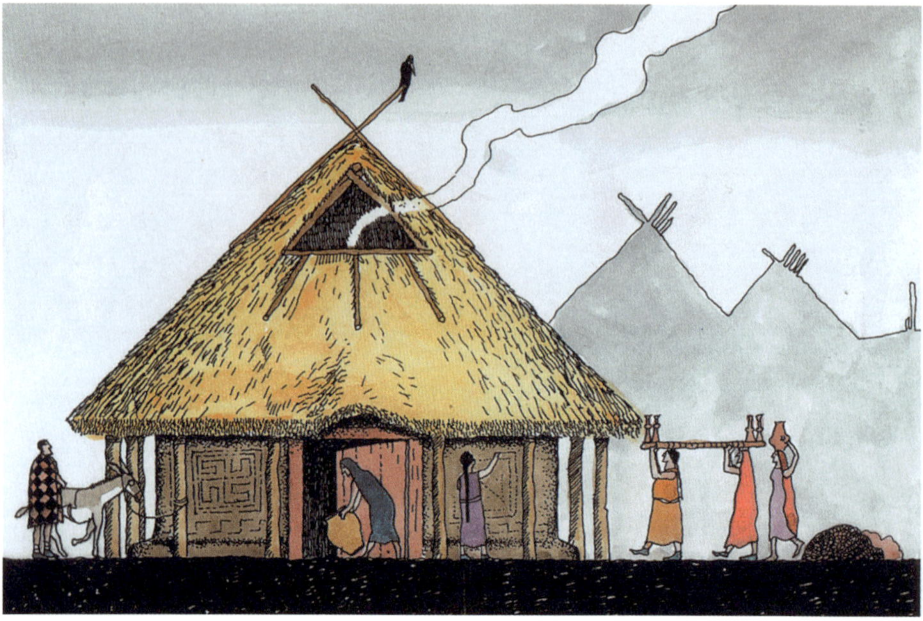

Reconstruction of the hut at Fidenae.

The Hut at Fidenae

Documentation of built-up areas is provided by the Iron Age hut (early Latial Period III, late 9th century BC) at Fidenae, one of Latium's oldest towns. Due to its position on the Tiber, bordering with Sabina and facing the Etruscan city of Veii, Fidenae was often at odds with Rome, which definitively conquered it in 426 BC. The structure, which was destroyed by fire, had a rectangular layout with its entrance on the west side preceded by a portico. The walls were built with the *pisè* technique (clay mixed with water, crushed ceramic and straw, and pressed in a formwork of wooden boards). The roof with four gables was held up by four internal pillars and a continuous line of external posts around the perimeter. At the centre of the interior space was a fireplace with a series of clay andirons. The entire north half was used for storage purposes, and was occupied by three large vases (or *doli*) and a smaller vase, which was filled with clay and buried in the floor. The museum presents a reconstruction of the hut (which has also been recreated in full scale on the excavation site), the organisation of the interior spaces and furnishings, and a selection of ceramics. Inside the hut, the remains of a small cat were found. The burnt skeleton exhibited in the showcase is particularly interesting because it offers the earliest known evidence of domestic cats in Italy.

to one of the community's family groups (North Group). The cremation tombs of adult males are placed at the centre, while the burial graves of the group's other members are arranged around them. An example of the division of roles between the community's members is provided by weaving activity, suggested in the grave goods by the presence of *fuseruole* (small spheres used on spindles) and spools, which symbolised the loom. This function was exclusively entrusted to young women. In Latial Period III (late 9th – 8th centuries BC), the traditional elements of funerary ideology were profoundly transformed. We know of a single group of tombs from this period (Group N), isolated at the centre of the necropolis. The ritual underlines the group's spatial concentration, which took precedence over the integrity of the individual burial places. For the first time the grave goods included life-sized weapons – which were now also present in the tombs of adult and elderly males – but also revealed differences in wealth. These novelties marked the emergence of a permanent social differentiation that would lead to the system of nobility and patronage in ancient Latin society. Towards the end of Period III, certain tombs appeared in Latium's necropolises that stood out with their exceptional signs of wealth and prestige, constituting a direct precedent for the princely tombs of the Orientalising period.
In the necropolis at Osteria dell'Osa, Tomb 600 belongs to this category. Reconstructed in bass-relief on the wall, the tomb is attributable on the basis of the materials to a Villanovan prince, probably originally from Veii but entirely integrated into his local society, where he retained the high status he enjoyed in his community of origin. In the era following the Orientalising (Latial period IVA-IVB, second half of the 8th – early 6th centuries BC), the tombs document a progressive consolidation of social differentiation. In the early stages of this period, certain burial places revealed tomb goods of notable affluence (Tomb 116), while in the final stage one encounters collective chamber tombs used by aristocratic families (Tomb 62). The necropolis at Castiglione – located near the Osteria dell'Osa necropolis and coeval with its earliest period – reveals a number of differences in the material culture and overall organisation.
Another exhibited complex is the necropolis of La Rustica, which can be identified with the ancient Latin town of Collatia. Situated along the ancient Via Collatina, La Rustica lies a short distance from the Aniene River, midway between Rome and Gabii. One of the smaller towns that developed in *Latium vetus* between the late Period IIB and the early Period III (circa 9th century BC), it enjoyed a strategic position on some of the major communication and trade routes via both land and river. The necropolis, located on high ground to the north of the built-up area, documents the same chronological periods. The oldest tombs offer the most extensive and comprehensive documentation for the later stage of Latial Period III (8th century BC). The burial places – which are mostly female – reveal tomb goods characterised by a remarkable level of affluence, as shown by tombs 81 and 238 present in the exhibition. The most numerous group of burial places can be dated to Latial Period IV (late 8th – early 6th centuries BC). The most important burial places are pseudo-chamber tombs (large quadrangular graves without an entrance and covered by wooden boards). The male Tomb 3 with chariot exhibited in the museum belongs to this type. (A.D.S.)

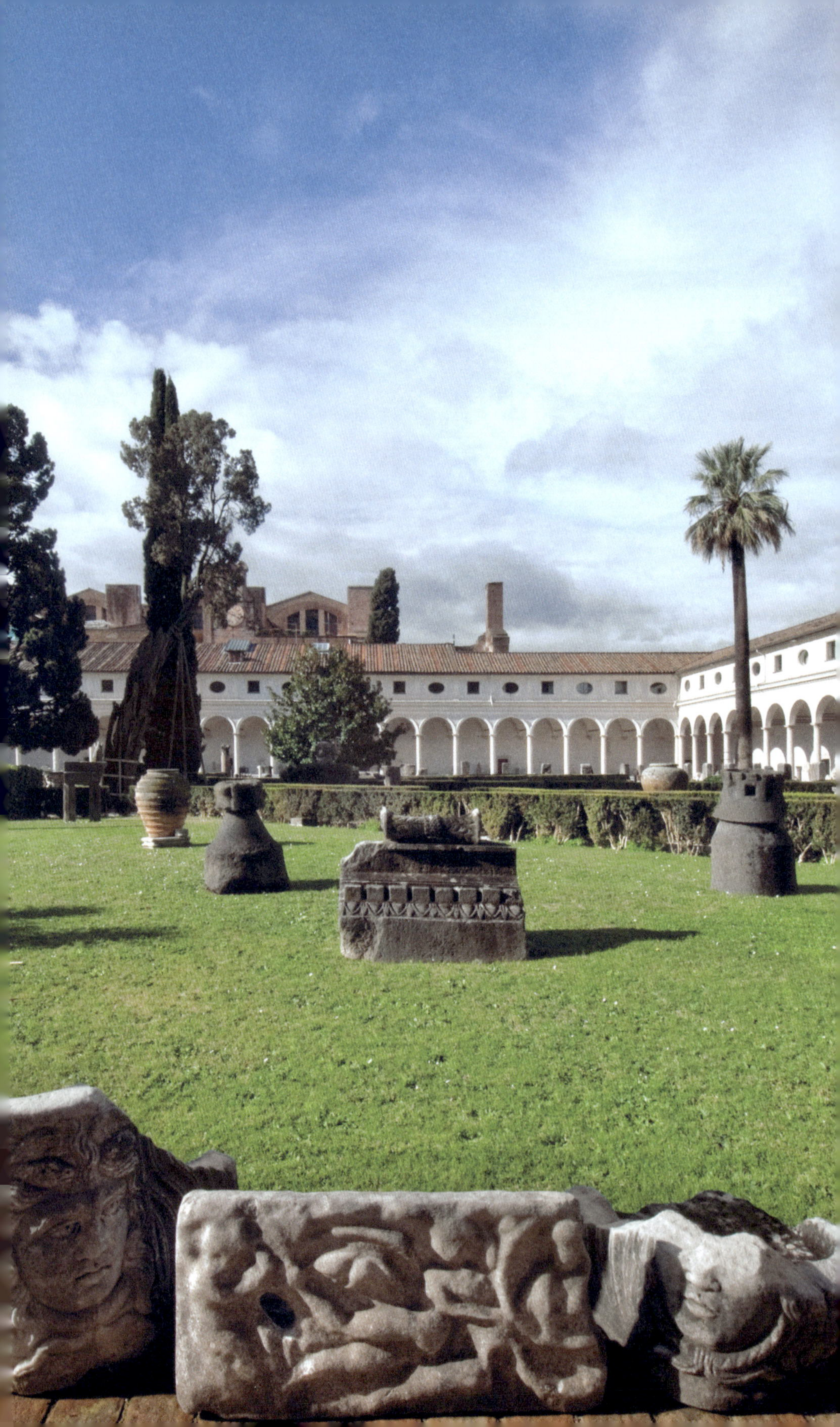

Michelangelo's Cloister

Emerging from the Entrance Hall we come to the Cloister of the Charterhouse of the Church of Santa Maria degli Angeli e dei Martiri.
The cloister is traditionally attributed to Michelangelo because it was to him that the task of converting the *frigidarium* of the Baths of Diocletian into a church in 1561 had been given. In fact the church and Charterhouse have a coherent design, but it is more likely that Michelangelo (who died in 1564) had merely suggested the layout and then entrusted the job to a pupil, Giacomo del Duca, who was involved in the work in at least the initial phase. This began in 1565 and was not completed until the beginning of 1600.
But the second floor of the cloister was only finished in 1676 and the fountain that stands at the centre of the garden was built in 1695. The models applied

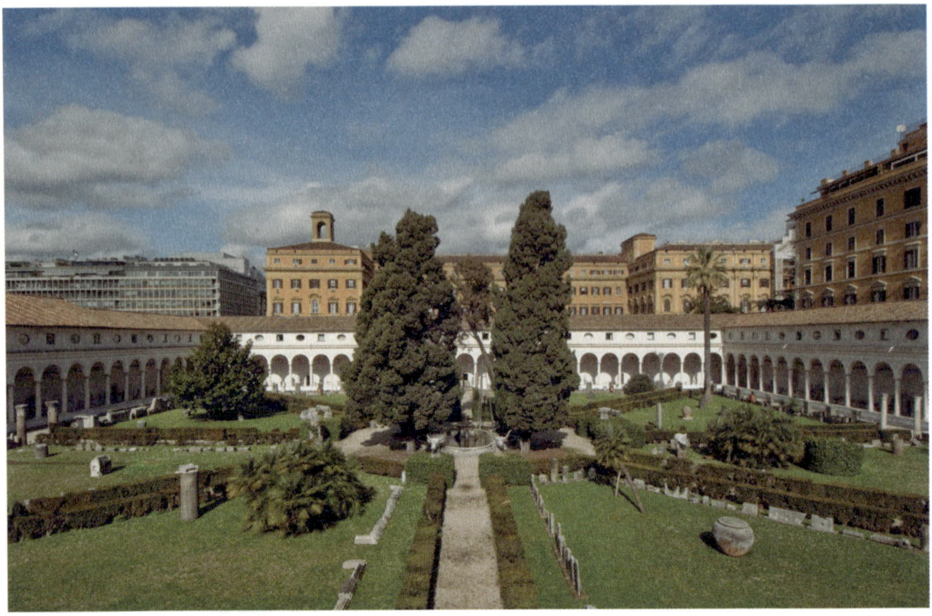

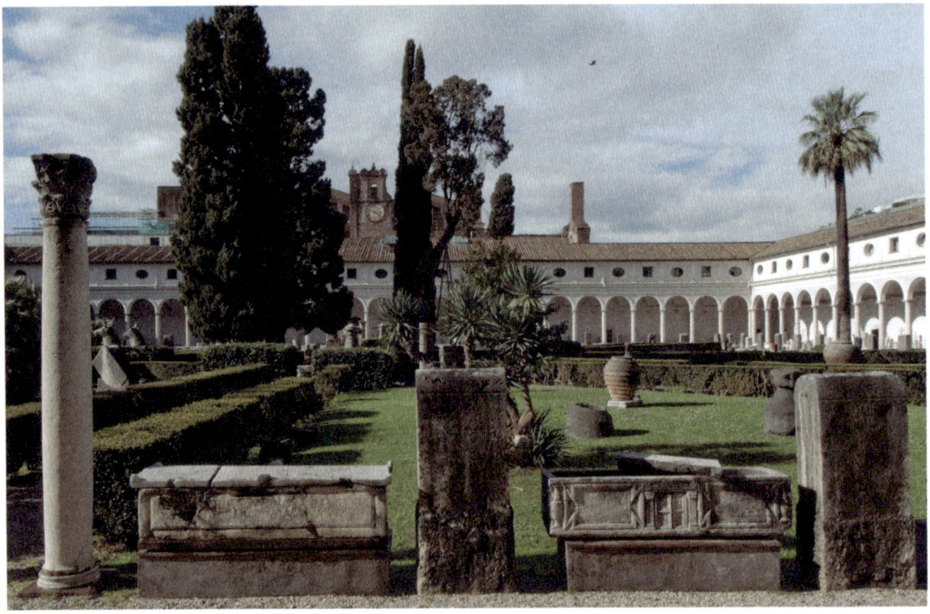

Page 44
Michelangelo's Cloister.

Views of Michelangelo's Cloister.

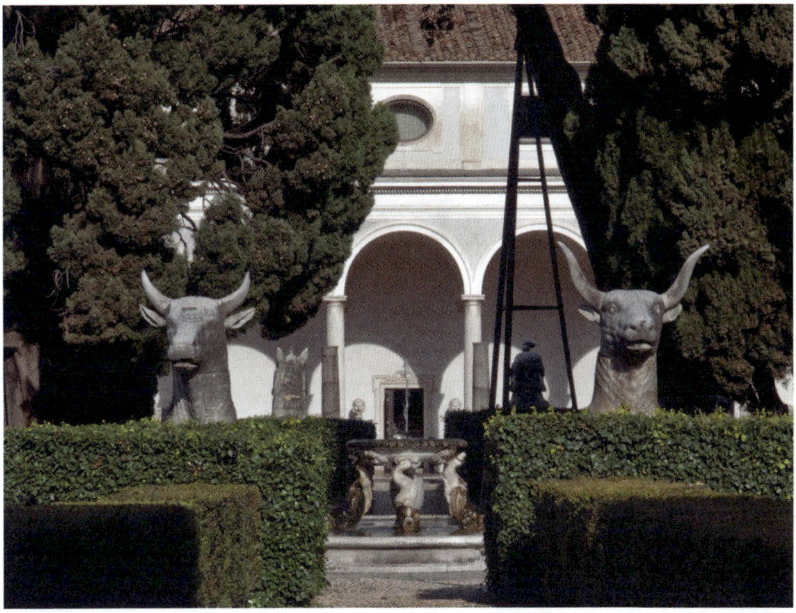

The central fountain and the colossal heads of animals around it.

in the cloister are those of Carthusian architecture, adapted to the Roman style of architecture of the late 16th century. The complex, which had undergone various alterations over the course of the centuries, was restored for the Jubilee of 2000, bringing it back to its original appearance and returning the plastering to its old colour. The cloister has been used to display exhibits since 1889, but the transfer of some sculptures to Palazzo Massimo alle Terme and Palazzo Altemps has modified the layout and new works have been set up in their place. Numerous statues, stelae and sarcophagi are arranged in the four wings; many of these are noteworthy works that illustrate the requirements of a middle- to upper-class clientele who wished to present an image in keeping with their social status. There are too many of them for us to mention more than the most significant. Other statues are located in the garden, for the most part colossal heads of animals (not all of them dating from antiquity) from Palazzo Valentini (near Trajan's Column), where they were found in 1586.

Wing I

Exiting on the right gives access to Wing I that houses some important sculptures: the headless statue wearing a lorica (mail shirt) found on the Via Praenestina, a statue of a man in heroic seminudity from San Giovanni Incarico and the beautiful 2nd-century-AD statue of a standing woman, probably a priestess of Ceres, holding ears of grain and poppies, i.e. the attributes of the goddess. The pair of seated headless statues from the Julio-Claudian period in the middle of the wing are of outstanding quality: coming from a sepulchral monument at Tor Pignattara, one is of a man dressed in a toga and the other of a draped woman, derived from a type used in the Hellenistic era for images of Tychai and of Muses. Of particular interest among

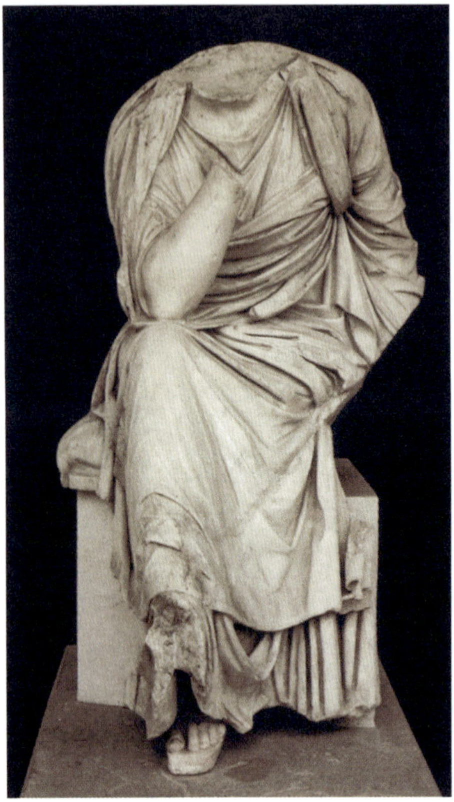

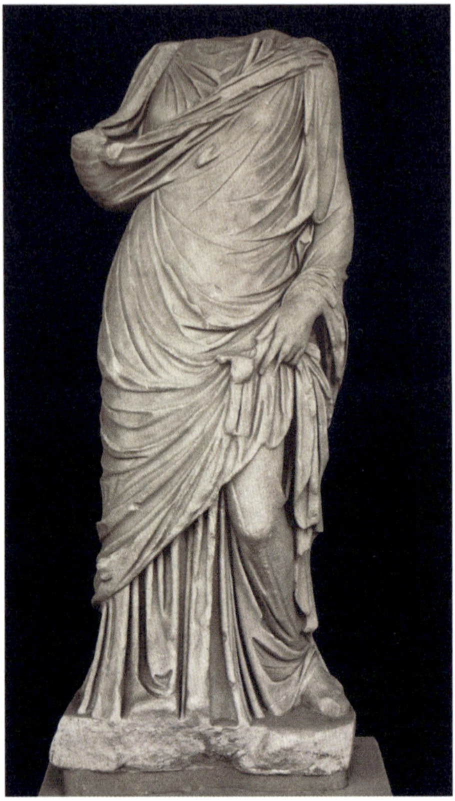

Tyche- or Muse-type funerary statue of a woman from the Via Casilina.

Priestess of Ceres from Porta Furba.

the funerary altars and sarcophagi on display are the altar of T. Aspulenus Carellianus, decorated with a rich series of decorative funerary motifs, and the sarcophagus of a child with a *Centauromachy* on the chest and a *Gigantomachy* on the lid.

Wing II

Wing II presents a wide variety of sarcophagi and allows us to appreciate the full range of their decorative repertoire. In many cases they are adorned with Dionysiac scenes in which the god is accompanied by a procession of satyrs and bacchantes (while the discovery of the sleeping Ariadne is depicted on the sarcophagus found in the church of Santi Nereo e Achilleo). On others we find the scheme of two winged figures holding an inscription or clipeus (medallion) with the bust of the deceased: on the 3rd-century-AD sarcophagus found on the Via Casilina two winged genii hold the clipeus, while beneath them are set Oceanus and Tellus and the image of the centaur Chiron educating Achilles is repeated on the sides. Among the sarcophagi with mythological scenes is one from Palazzo Caucci, just after the middle of the wing, illustrating the myth of Medea, from the dispatch of poisoned gifts to Creusa to her flight, after killing her sons, on the chariot drawn by dragons. A series of smaller sarcophagi belong to children and are usually decorated with erotes as a reminder of their youth. At the end of the wing are set two imposing sarcophagi from the late 1st century AD that depict their owners lying on their funeral beds (*klini*).

Wing III

A series of altars and bases of statues that were dedicated to numerous deities and the genius of the emperor by the *equites singulares* (imperial horse guards) at the time of their discharge are located at the beginning of Wing III. They are followed by funerary altars, some of them adorned with figurative decorations like the small altar depicting the brothers Biton and Cleobis taking the place of the oxen to pull their mother's cart all the way to Delphi. After these come numerous funerary reliefs with portraits of the deceased and some statues, including a sleeping boy with a hood holding a lantern inspired by Hellenistic genre sculpture. The elegant funerary relief representing a centaur carrying off a nymph comes from the Via Praenestina, while next to it is set the remarkable headless statue of Aphrodite standing, belonging to the type known as the Venus Callipyge.

Wing IV

Wing IV houses a number of portraits and works of ideal sculpture, copies and reworkings of Greek statues used as idols for worship and more frequently to decorate gardens, houses, villas and public buildings. There are numerous gods like Dionysius (represented drunk and leaning on a pillar from which hangs a goatskin), Aphrodite, Hera and Diana, whose cult is also illustrated by two decorated

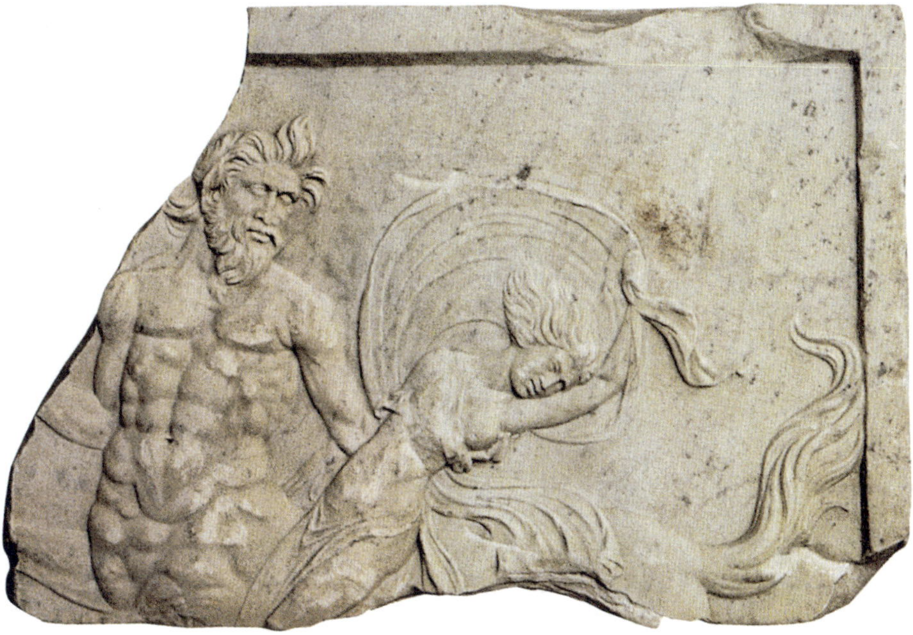

Relief from the Via Praenestina with a centaur carrying off a nymph.

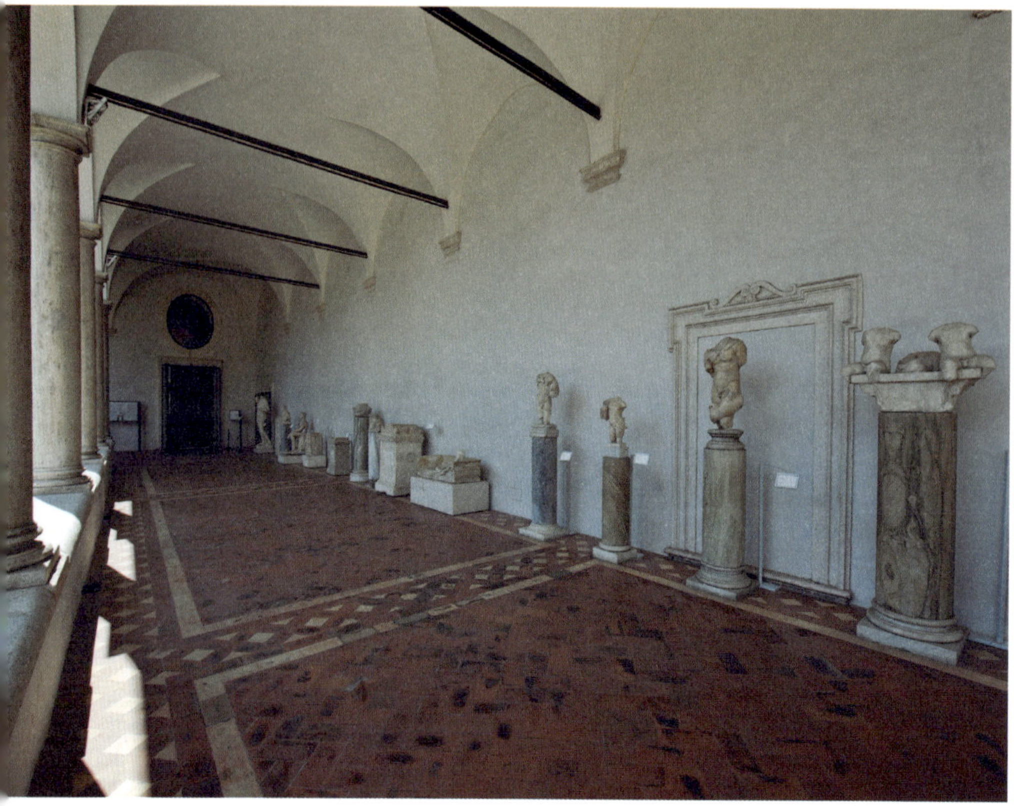

A wing of Michelangelo's Cloister.

altars dedicated to the goddess. In the middle of the wing, the statue representing an elderly fisherman is a Roman copy inspired by models developed in the Hellenistic era by the "realistic" current active chiefly in Alexandria. A short distance away stands a small statuary group with Ganymede and Jupiter's eagle perched on a rock. Unusual are the "sofa" capital on which two boys are seated and the small votive sculpture representing a ship surmounted by the base of a column, probably vowed by a sailor for his return. At the end of the wing it is worth singling out two statues of Hercules, one standing and one seated, inspired by the models of Polyclitus, and one of an athlete from the Via Ostiensis. Onto this wing faces the inner part of the first door of the cloister, decorated with an oil painting of the Carthusian monk Foulquois, executed by Filippo Balbi in 1855. Father of Pope Clement IV, Foulquois took vows after losing his wife and died in 1265. (M.C.)

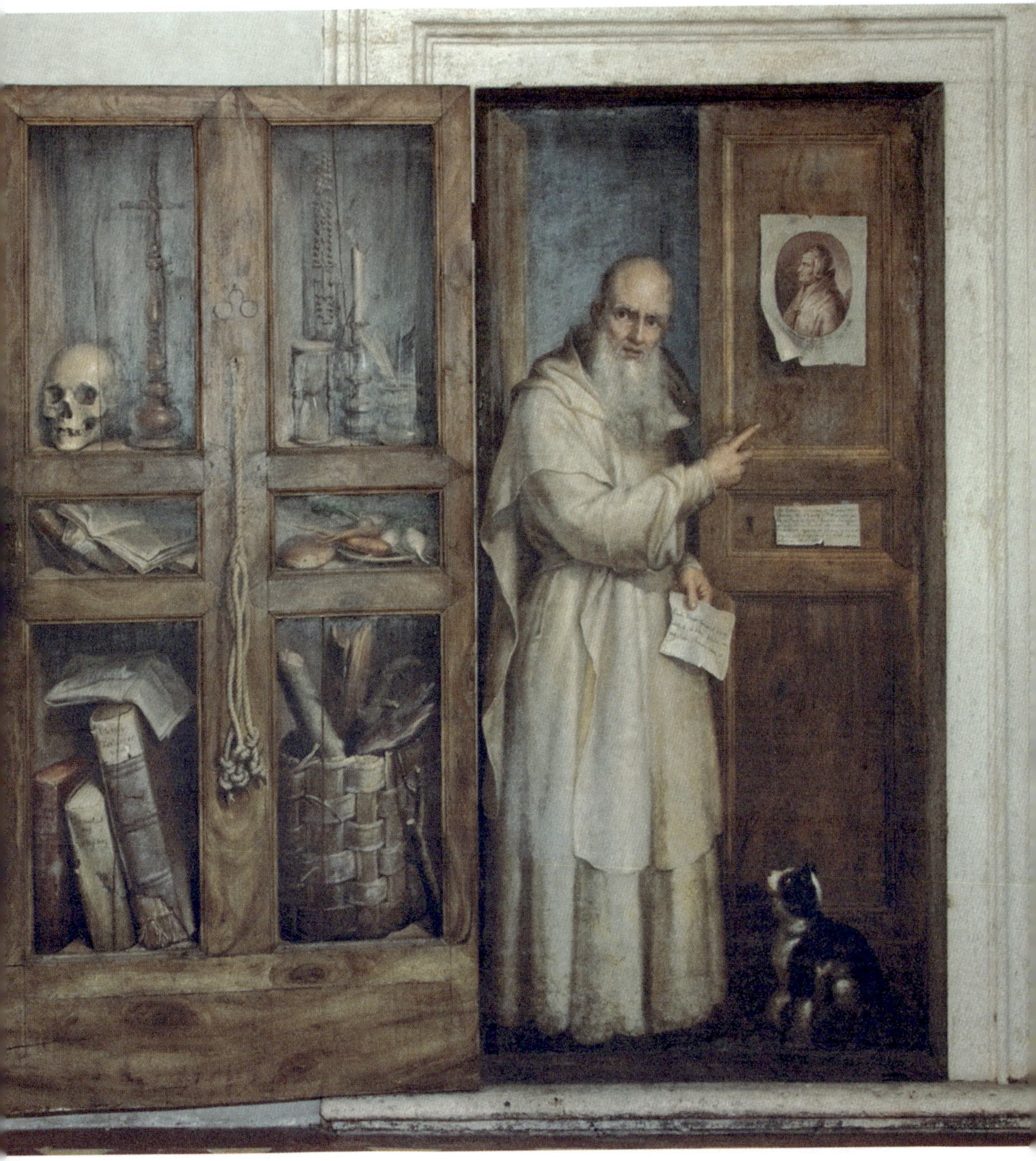

The door painted
with a picture of the
Carthusian monk Foulquois.

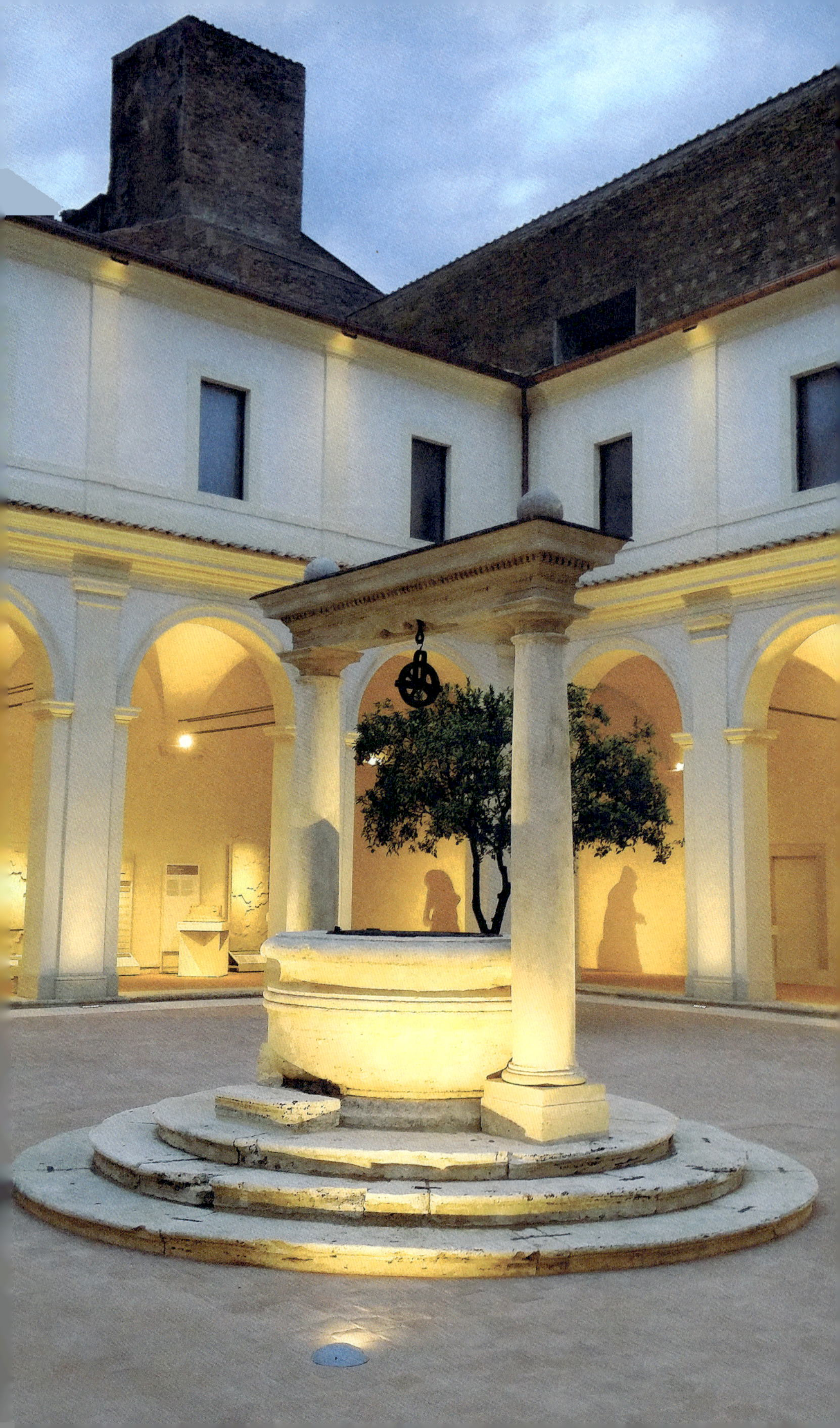

The Small Cloister of the Charterhouse of Santa Maria degli Angeli

The Small Cloister of the Charterhouse of Santa Maria degli Angeli, or the *claustrino* as it was called in the 16th-century chronicle by Matteo Catalani, occupies almost a third of the large uncovered pool, natatio, of the Baths of Diocletian. The cloister, built on the Roman monument as an integral part of the Charterhouse, risked demolition in the early 20th century, in the name of the archaeological restoration of the Baths' structures. The cloister's long and difficult construction began in the second half of the 16th century, when Pope Pius IV Medici (1559-65), ordered the transformation of the central part of the Baths to create the Basilica of Santa Maria degli Angeli (Papal bull of 27 July 1561). Work on its construction continued throughout the 17th century and beyond.

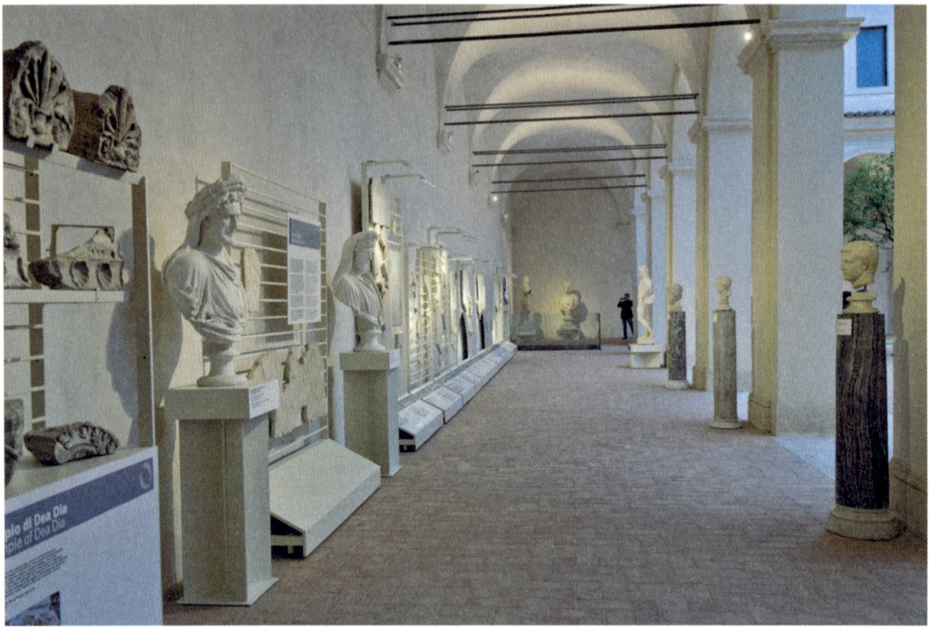

Page 52
The cloister after the recent restoration, with a late-16th-century circular travertine well set at the centre of the court. The architectural elements are made with reused materials.

The southeast wing of the cloister.

The cloister has a square plan with sides of circa 40 metres. Divided into two levels, its ground floor has porticoes marked by columns of the Tuscan order, and ambulatories with six bays covered by cross vaulting. The closed upper floor, meanwhile, is punctuated with slender, subtly projecting pilasters. The sobriety and simplification of the architectural order, such as the treatment of elements in imitation travertine, place the cloister's design within the typical compositional and stylistic schemes of late-16th-century Rome. The restoration has brought to light the former recognisability, prestige and evocative beauty of the cloister, which has been architecturally and historically central to the life of the Charterhouse. After a long period of neglect it has regained the original colours of its surfaces, along with its monumental value.

The ambulatories host a display of the main documents pertaining to Roman religion, and in particular of the cults refounded by Augustus within the scope of his religious policy aimed at restoring ancient ceremonies for ideological purposes. The first three wings of the cloister present the records of the Arval Brothers, a priestly college made up of 12 high-ranking figures. The annual accounts of their activities not only constitute a unique source of information regarding sacred rituals, but also offer insight into many historical and political events in the first three centuries of the Roman Empire. In the last wing, meanwhile, one finds the reconstruction of two large marble pillars containing accounts of the *Ludi saeculares* announced by Augustus and Septimius Severus. The texts describe the various stages of the rituals which celebrated the new *saeculum* (see p. 57). Furthermore, the exhibition includes two important inscriptions: the *Lex Familiae Silvani* and the *Lex collegi salutaris Dianae et Antinoi*, with the statutes of confraternities for worshipers of the god Silvanus and of Diana and Antinous, the young man adored and divinised by Hadrian.

The Arval Brothers and the Sacred Grove of *Dea Dia*

The sacred grove of Dea Dia, or the *lucus Deae Diae*, was located near the place that is today occupied by the Magliana Railway Station, along the current motorway to Fiumicino, level with the fifth mile of the ancient via Campana. *Dea Dia*, the goddess "of the shining sky", was worshipped to guarantee the fertility of the fields -*arva*-, so that they would produce cereals -*fruges*- through her benevolent light. This ancient cult was re-established by Augustus, whose policy of reviving archaic religions was combined with a fervent activity of restoring temples and shrines. The brotherhood of the Fratres Arvales was composed of 12 priests headed by a *magister*, and its origins were closely associated with the myth of Rome's foundation. Indeed, according to tradition, the first priests were the sons of *Acca Larentia*, the woman who, together with her shepherd-husband Faustulus, raised Romulus and Remus after taking them away from the care of a she-wolf. With the death of *Acca Larentia*'s 12th son, Romulus took his place and declared himself the 12th brother, subsequently founding the brotherhood. Legend recounts that Romulus himself chose the priesthood's emblem, a chaplet or garland of plaited ears of wheat which the priests wore on their heads during ceremonies. In recruiting the first members of the brotherhood, Augustus chose senators representing Rome's oldest families who had fought against each other during the civil wars. He thus gathered them around him in a confraternity whose members were called *fratres*, or brothers. The brotherhood's main function was to celebrate the festival of *Dea Dia*, a three-day sacrifice held in May. The Arval Brothers also performed numerous votive sacrifices for various occasions, such as the traditional vows –*vota*– on 3 January, pronounced at the start of every year on the Capitoline Hill for the good health of the emperor.

The Inscriptions

In the Roman world priests drew up annual accounts to record the religious services celebrated and the decisions made. These reports or minutes were written on *codices*, or wooden boards covered with wax, which were deposited in archives and reserved for the exclusive use of the priests. Along with the *codices*, the Arval Brothers also carved copies of all their accounts on marble, constituting a unique testimony of about 150 inscriptions covering circa three centuries, from 21/20 BC to 304 AD.

The texts were carved on marble slabs cladding the buildings in the sacred grove, and on each occasion they were adapted to the architectural structures, as in the arches of the Neronian period. Probably due to a lack of space, by the end of the 2nd century AD the accounts were being carved at the bottom of older slabs to fill every empty space, without respecting the documents' chronological order (the account of the year 213 was added at the bottom of the slab dating from 155, and that of 219 at the base of the slab from 90). Subsequently, pieces of furniture were also used, such a tabletop (for the account of 218) or the leg of the same table (for the account of 220). The first documents were very short and only listing essential details about the brotherhood's members and the record of the *indictio*, or the official announcement of the date for the most important ceremony in honour of Dea Dia. As a moveable festival, this ceremony could fall on the 17, 19 and 20 May, or on the 27, 29 and 30 May. These documents were followed by a calendar, which also included the list of consuls and praetors. As of the 1st century AD there was an increase in the amount of data recorded, and the structure of the accounts began a gradual transformation that culminated in the documents of the 3rd century. In this period, the descriptions of the ceremonies were enriched with meticulous details such as the texts of prayers, the lyrics of the ritual hymn, descriptions of the food eaten at feasts, the robes worn during sacrifices, and much more. (C.C.)

The Secular Games

The Secular Games *-ludi saeculares-* were celebrations held at the end of each *saeculum*, a period not determined by an exact number of years, but by a man's maximum life expectancy. According to the Neopythagorean theory, humankind was regenerated every 440 years, divided into four periods of 110 years, a succession of four eras that began with the Golden Age. Perhaps harking back to this theory, Augustus decided to stage the largest ceremony ever organised (with help from the young jurist *C. Ateius Capito*), in an effort to present himself as the initiator of the new Golden Age. The year of the celebration was fixed for 17 BC, based on the sequence of *ludi* that had been celebrated previously. Under the direction of the priestly college consisting of the *quindecemviri sacris faciundis*, headed by Augustus, the *ludi quinti* (fifth games) were celebrated as the first games of a new cycle. The sixth games in this cycle were to be held in 88 AD, and the seventh games in 204 AD. The *ludi saeculares* lasted three days and three nights, during which sacrifices, staged performances and symbolic banquets *-sellisternia-* were held, where the emblems of female divinities were placed on chairs in front of tables full of lavish offerings. The great celebration ended the era of the preceding generation, while invoking the help of the divinities for the new one. The aim was to ensure healthy descendents, which was the only guarantee for the future well-being of the Roman state. Accordingly, the oracle included sacrifices to the divinities of procreation, and an important role in the celebration of rituals was ascribed to children and married women of high lineage. The children represented the new generation, and sang the sacred hymn at the closing ceremony. The matrons made a display of their motherly responsibilities and recited the secular prayer assisted by the Vestal Virgins and the emperor, who led the *quindecemviri*. A few days before the celebrations began, torches, sulphur and pitch *-suffimenta-* were distributed to the citizens by the *quindecemviri* for purification rites. Afterwards, the citizens would bring *fruges* (wheat, barley and fava beans) to the priests as a contribution to the rewards for the games' participants. Nocturnal sacrifices were offered at the Tarentum on the Campus Martius, near the Tiber at the level of today's Ponte Vittorio Emanuele II. Daytime sacrifices, meanwhile, were offered on the Capitoline and Palatine hills. During the night of 31 May and 1 June, sacrifices were offered to the Moirai, the divinities of destiny. The sacrifices consisted in nine black ewes and nine black she-goats, which were entirely burned. Each night, open-air shows were performed on simple stages with spectators remaining standing. Shortly before dawn, the matrons celebrated *sellisternia* on the Capitoline Hill in honour of Juno Regina. At dawn on 1 June on the Capitoline Hill, numerous oxen were sacrificed to Jupiter, and immediately after, plays lasting three days began in a theatre located on the bank of the Tiber. During the night of 1 and 2 June, a sacrifice was offered to the Eileithyiai, the goddesses of childbirth, consisting of nine plain biscuits *-popana-*, nine cakes *-liba-* and nine sweets *-pthoes-*. During the day, a cow was offered to Juno Regina, again on the Capitoline Hill, after which the matrons recited a supplication to the goddess. During the night of 2 and 3 June, a sacrifice was dedicated to Mother Earth: a pregnant black sow was entirely consumed by the fire as the matrons celebrated *sellisternia* for Juno and Diana. The following day, on the Palatine Hill, biscuits, cakes and sweets were offered to Apollo and Diana. Immediately afterwards, 27 boys and 27 girls intoned the secular hymn on the Palatine Hill and then on the Capitoline Hill. The hymn was composed in Augustus's times by the poet Horace. Races at the circus brought the celebration to a close, followed by another seven days of theatrical performances and circus races, starting on 5 June. (C.C.)

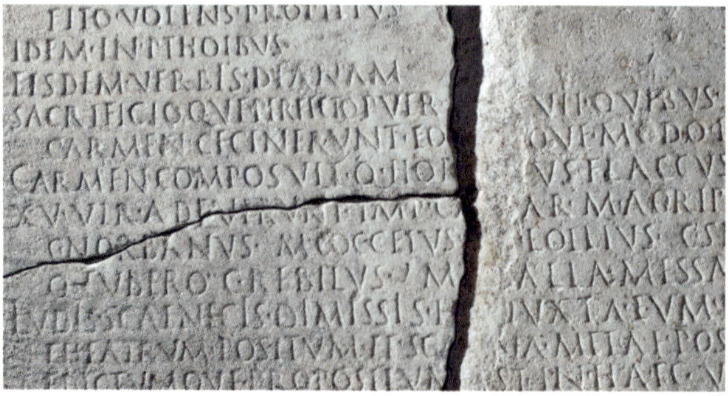

Ludi saeculares, fragment of the inscription by Augustus dating from 17 BC, detail where Horace is mentioned as the author of the *carmen saeculare* sung on that occasion.

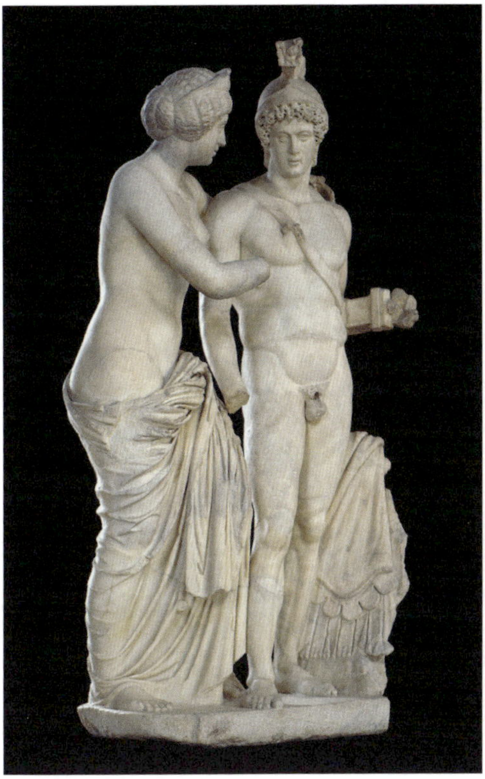

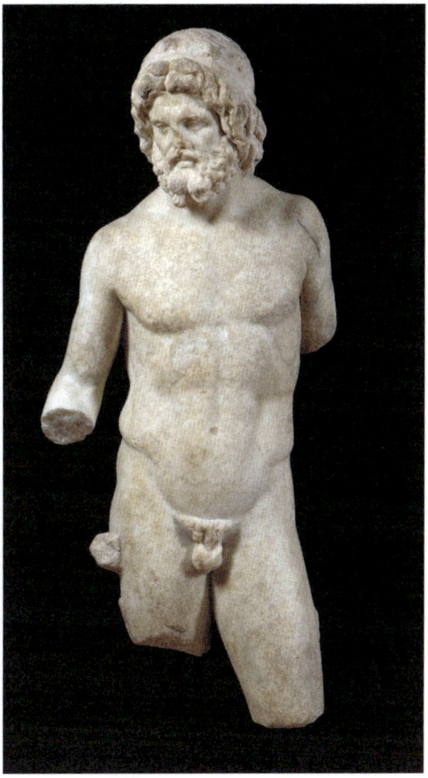

Numerous sculptures offer us images of the characters and divinities mentioned in the documents. Of these, notable examples include a portrait of Octavian, created prior to his being awarded the title of Augustus; a statue of Jupiter Aegiochus originating from the Viminal Hill; a portrait statue dating from the late 2nd century AD, probably for funeral purposes, of a woman with a veiled head; and lastly a sculptural group with portraits of two wealthy members of society portrayed as Mars and Venus, together with a statue originating from the Roman Forum portraying a Vestalis Maxima, the oldest of the priestesses devoted to the cult of Vesta, the goddess of the hearth. In addition, recently found works are displayed for the first time after being discovered between 2010 and 2011 at Morena, in excavations carried out between the 7th and 8th mile of the ancient Via Latina. The dig uncovered the remains of a large villa used for residential and agricultural production purposes. In its oldest parts, the villa dates back to the mid-Republican period, and it remained in use at least until the 5th century AD. The decorative scheme, which above all references the cultural panorama of the 2nd century AD, features portraits of emperors in the villa's rooms set aside for receiving and entertaining guests, and sculptures for the garden and private spaces. In the Late Antique period, some works were removed and carefully buried on a bed of brick fragments in the central basin of the atrium –*impluvium*– while others were inten-

Group of Mars and Venus with portrait heads, from Ostia.

Statue of Zeus, from Rome, villa on the Via Anagnina.

Portrait of Augustus, from Rome, Via di Massa San Giuliano.

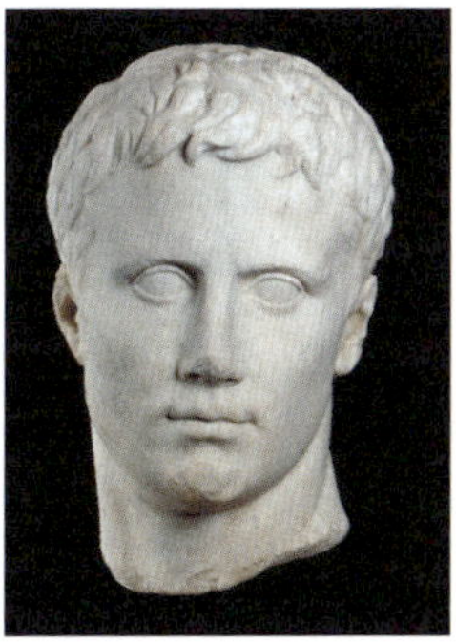

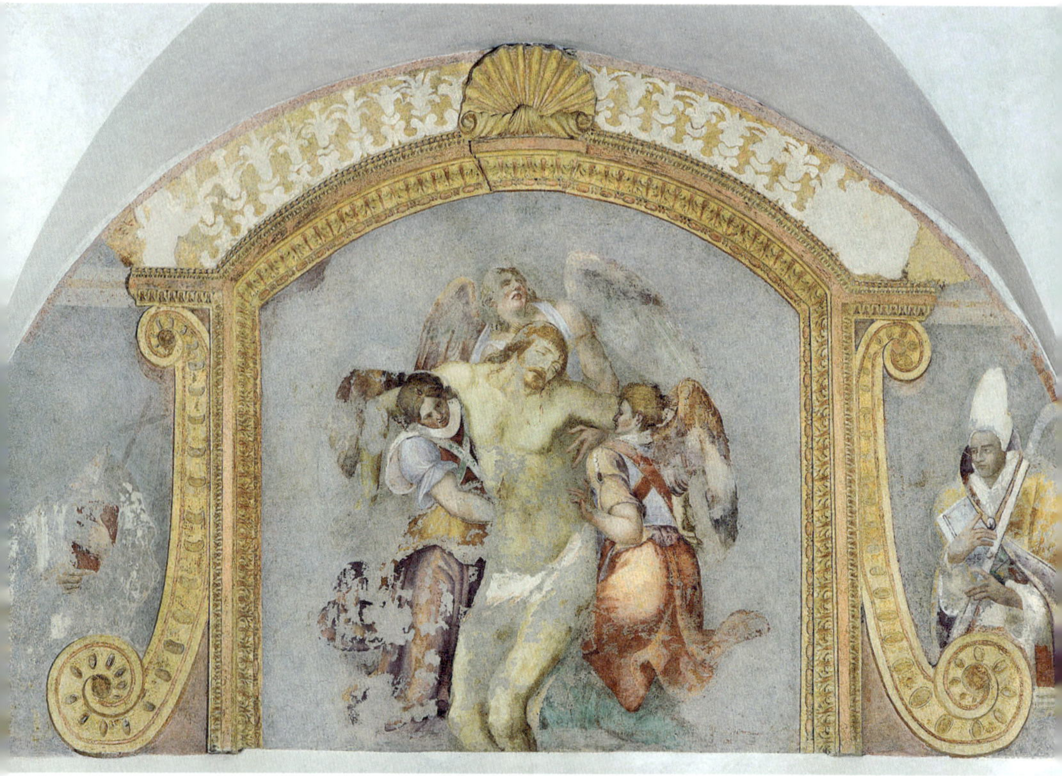

"Angels of Mercy"
© ph. Domenico Ventura.

tionally broken up and later buried in the vicinity of the *doliarium*.

Finally, in the last bay of the cloister's northeast ambulatory, a decorative stucco moulding frames a fresco portraying dead Christ supported by three angels, commonly known as "Angels of Mercy". To the right of the fresco, Pope Pius IV (1559 - 1565), and on the left, Saint Bruno of Cologne, founder of the Carthusian Order. The work is ascribable to the School of Daniele da Volterra, between 1565 and 1577. (C.B. - C.C.)

Dedicatory Inscription of the Baths of Diocletian

The inscription records that Diocletian and Maximian, *Augusti seniores* and fathers of the emperors and Caesars, together with the Augusti Constantius and Maximian, and with the Caesars Severus and Maximinus, dedicated the auspicious Baths of Diocletian to their Romans –*suis Romanis*. Upon his return to Rome from Africa, Maximian commissioned the Thermae and consecrated them to his co-emperor Diocletian, defined as his brother. Maximian purchased many buildings –*coemptis aedificiis*– to construct this huge and mighty work –*pro tanti operis magnitudine*– and furnish it with all manner of ornament –*omni cultu perfectas*. The full text is known thanks to a transcription made between the 8th and 9th centuries by an anonymous pilgrim. The transcription was preserved in a manuscript at Einsiedeln Abbey, Switzerland. Discovered in various periods and places around the area of the Baths, the fragments are not homogeneous in their style of workmanship or type of writing. The inscription was certainly drafted in more than one copy and displayed in different areas of the monumental complex, as confirmed by three other fragments of the inscription that are partially identical with the ones displayed here. Construction work on the Baths of Diocletian, the largest ever built in antiquity, began in 298 AD, upon Maximian's return from Africa, and was completed in less than eight years, in 306 AD, the year of Constantius's death.

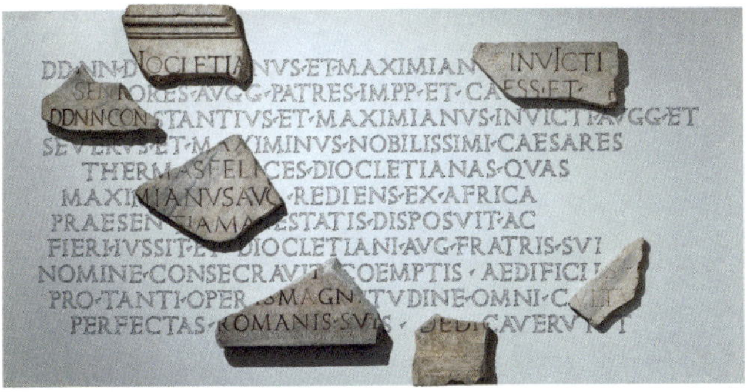

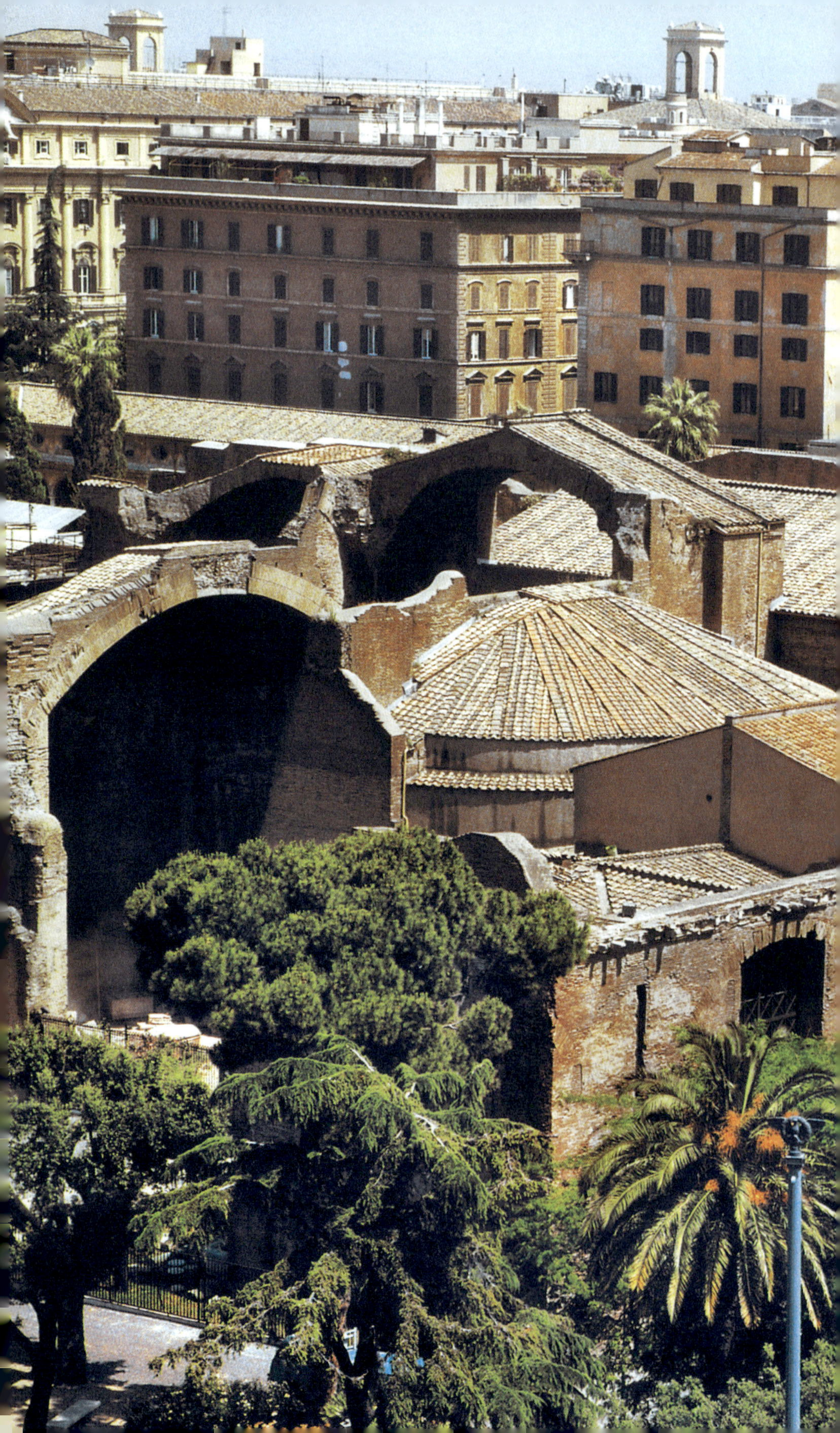

The Archaeological Tour

The archaeological tour leads through the spaces of the Baths of Diocletian. The *tepidarium* and the *frigidarium* constitute the vestibule and central body of the Basilica of Santa Maria degli Angeli e dei Martiri, while the remains of the *calidarium* can be recognised on the facade. Some of these have been incorporated into Santa Maria degli Angeli e dei Martiri, where the apse of the *caldarium* (on the facade), the *tepidarium* and the large *frigidarium* can be recognised. The Church of San Bernardo is also built in one of the circular rooms of the outer enclosure. On the other hand some of the Aule delle Olearie, or Oil Warehouses, the largest public work carried out by Clement XIII in order to ensure an efficient supply of oil to Rome, are part of the museum; they stand to the right of the Basilica of Santa Maria degli Angeli. Finally the museum also includes the so-called Octagonal Hall and the adjacent Hall of Sant'Isidoro.

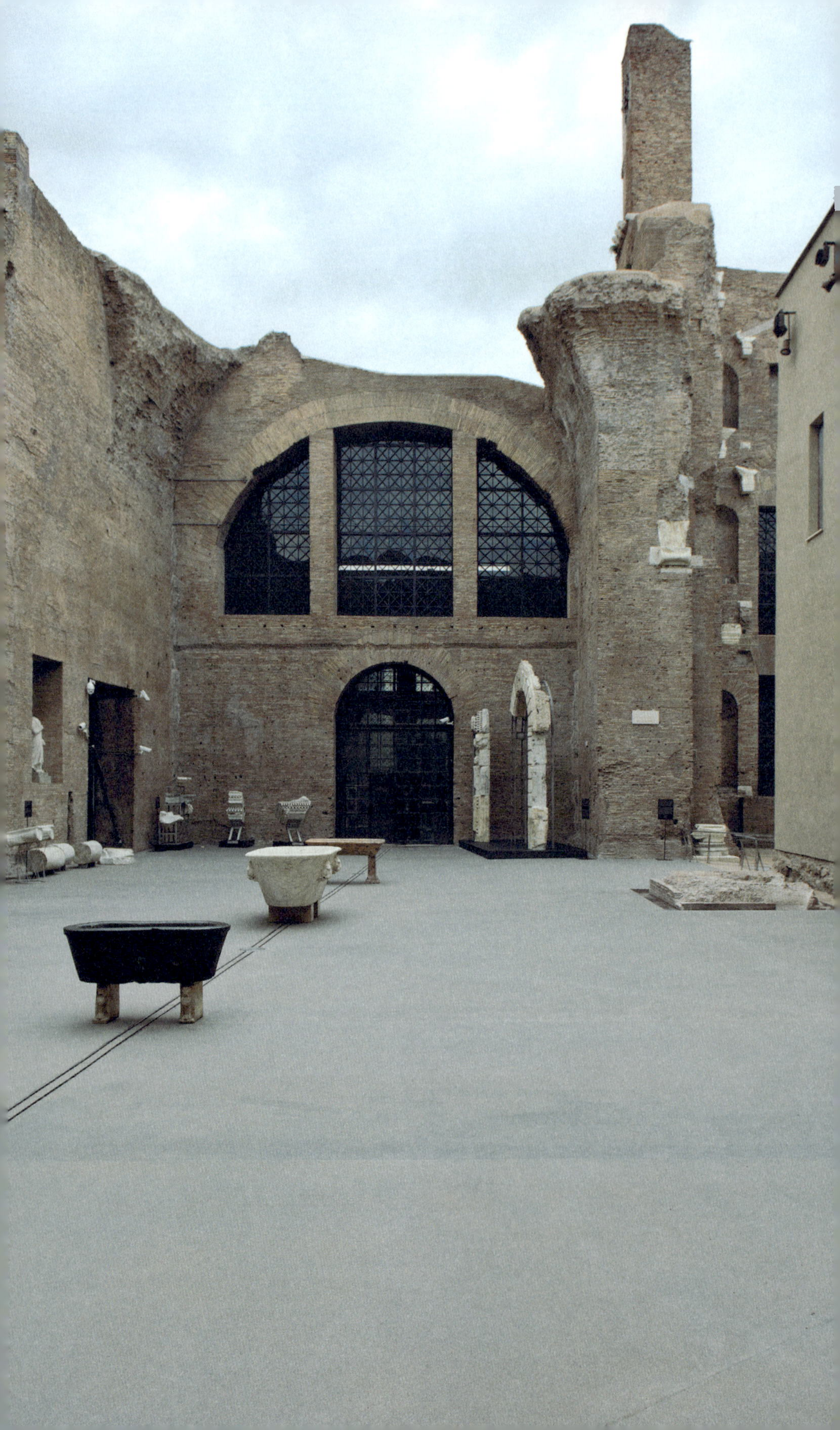

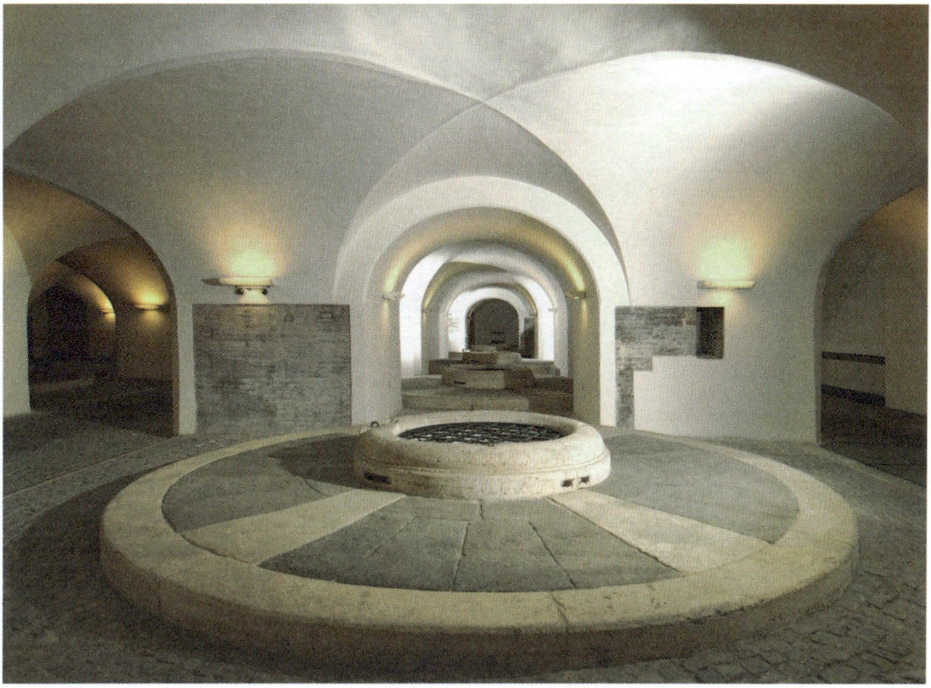

The latter is a small square room roofed with a cross vault that was annexed to the granary called the Annona in 1640, before being converted in 1754 into the Chapel of Sant'Isidoro in Thermis, of which only the facade remains today. The series of large halls (I-XI) of the Baths has been part of the museum since 1911, when the great archaeological exhibition was staged there in 1911. The various halls have been progressively restored and rearranged to make space for the collections of materials never before exhibited.

Page 60
The Baths of Diocletian seen from above.

Hall VIII: bottom right, the monumental portal of the Charterhouse of Santa Maria degli Angeli.

The *Olearie papali* (Oil Warehouses).

Hall VIII

This large hall (measuring 44 x 20 metres) was covered at either end by barrel vaults, one of which is partially preserved. The central part was covered by impressive groin vaults, which are today indicated only by markings on the floor. The hall overlooked the short side of the *natatio* with a front punctuated by two majestic columns, the lower parts of which are preserved. These pillars supported the vaults and were alternated by a row of architraved columns. Four basins used for lime production were discovered in the hall's floor. To make the slaked lime, pieces of marble were pried away from the architectural decoration of the structure and baked in ovens before being cooled in the water-filled basins.

The hall includes a display of architectural elements belonging to the Baths: the fragments of architrave, a column, the base and Ionic capital probably belonged to the front of the *natatio* opposite the monumental facade. The capital, datable between the mid-4th and early 5th centuries AD, provides evidence of the Baths' restoration shortly before their aban-

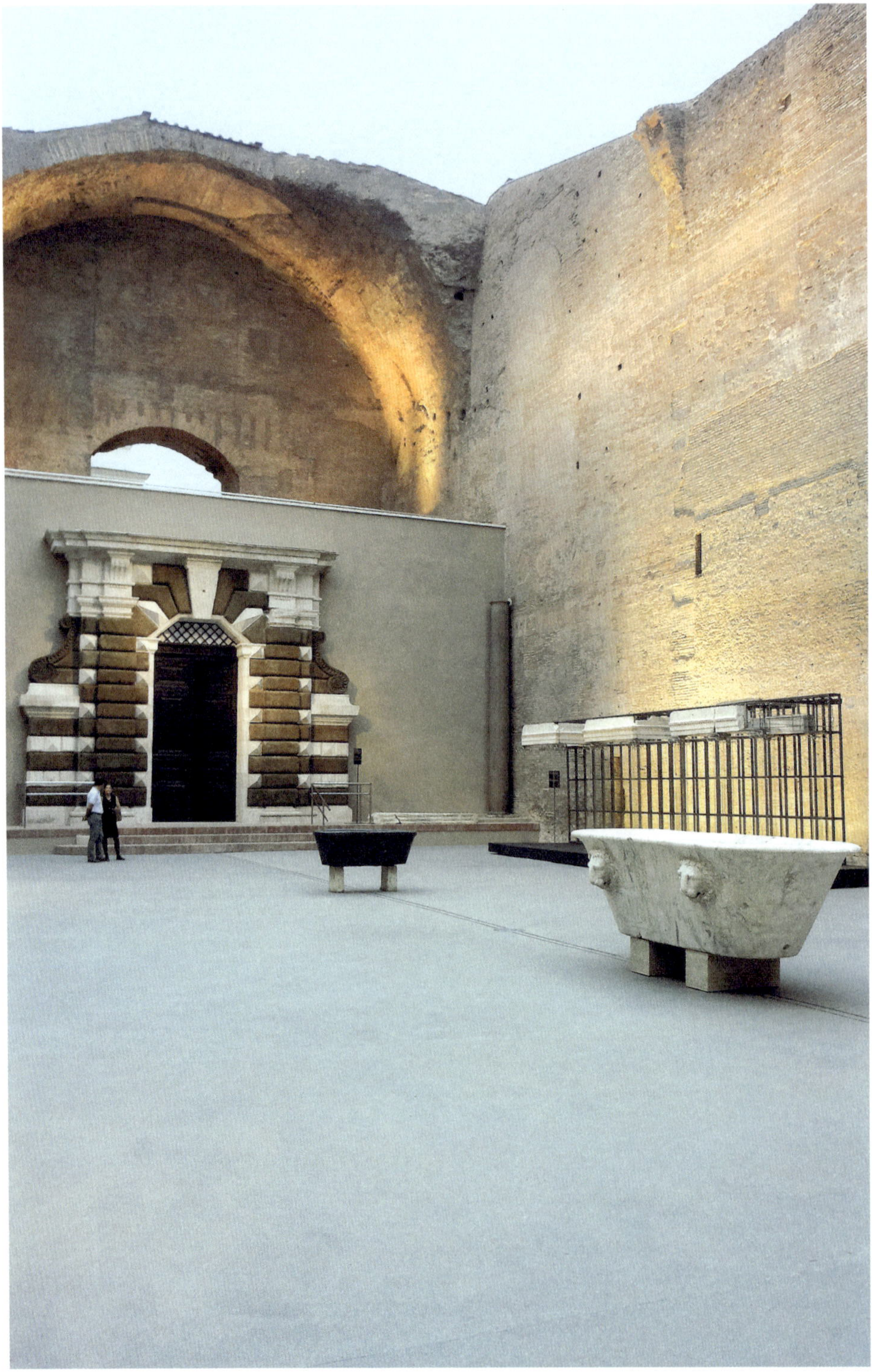

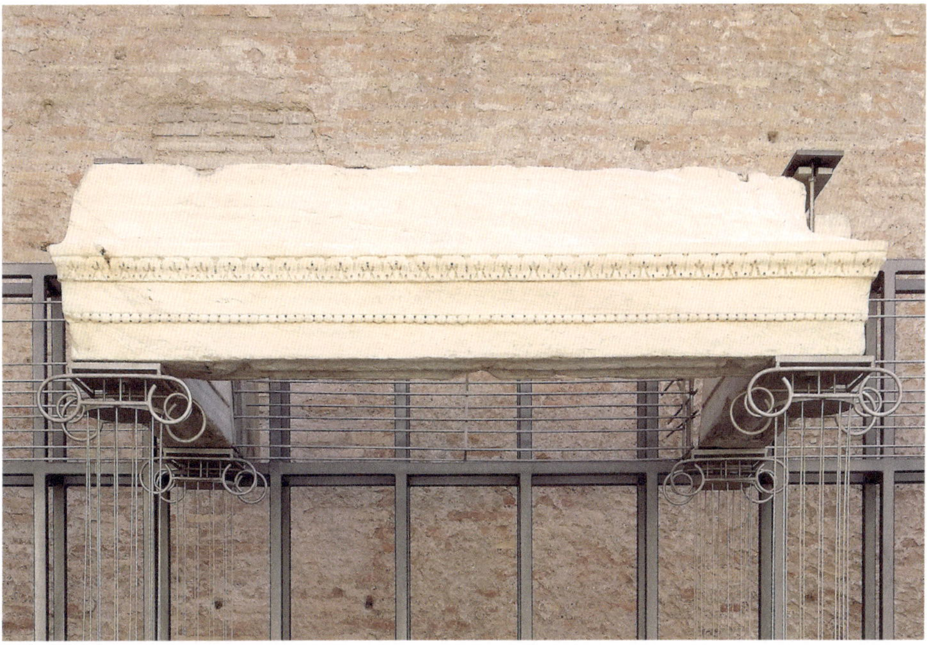

donment. The monumental portal, reconstructed at the back of the room, formed the entrance to the Charterhouse of Santa Maria degli Angeli. The marble ashlars that compose it were made by reworking architectural elements from the Baths of Diocletian. Specifically, an Ionic capital can be recognised along with parts of a cornice with *ovuli* (egg-shaped ornaments) and dentils from the spectacular facade of the *natatio*. The portal clearly testifies to the progressive spoliation of the Baths' decorations, carried out during the construction of the Charterhouse and ending with the extensive use of the marble to produce lime. In the late 19th century, when the monks abandoned the Charterhouse after the Italian unification, the gateway became the entrance to a hospice for poor blind people, the "Ospizio Margherita di Savoia", and subsequently to the museum. (C.B.)

Natatio

The large pool –*natatio*– had a surface area of about 4000 square metres and a depth of around 1 metre. The bottom and walls were clad with marble slabs from Luni, which are still partially preserved and indicated by the flooring that reproduces the sizes of the ancient slabs. The pool reflected the imposing monumental facade, which reproduced those found in the scenes of theatres. It is punctuated by four colossal recesses, two rectangular and two semicircular, which are alternated to the sides of the large entrance which once linked the *natatio* with the *frigidarium*. The front was composed of columns that framed *aediculae* and niches with statues. The surfaces were clad with coloured marble and mosaics to create extraordinary polychrome effects. Today the facade is interrupted by the apse of the Basilica of Santa Maria degli Angeli, which incorporates the large entrance and part of the *natatio*. In the late 16th century the Small Cloister of the Charterhouse was built in the pool, and it occupies about a third of the natatio's surface. (C.B.)

Hall VIII; at the back, the 16th-century rusticated-ashlar portal which once decorated the entrance to Villa Panzani near the present-day Largo di Santa Susanna. In 1907 it was dismantled and reconstructed here in 1911 for the extensive archaeological exhibition celebrating the 50th anniversary of Italian unification.

Architrave originating from the facade of the *natatio* opposite the monumental facade.

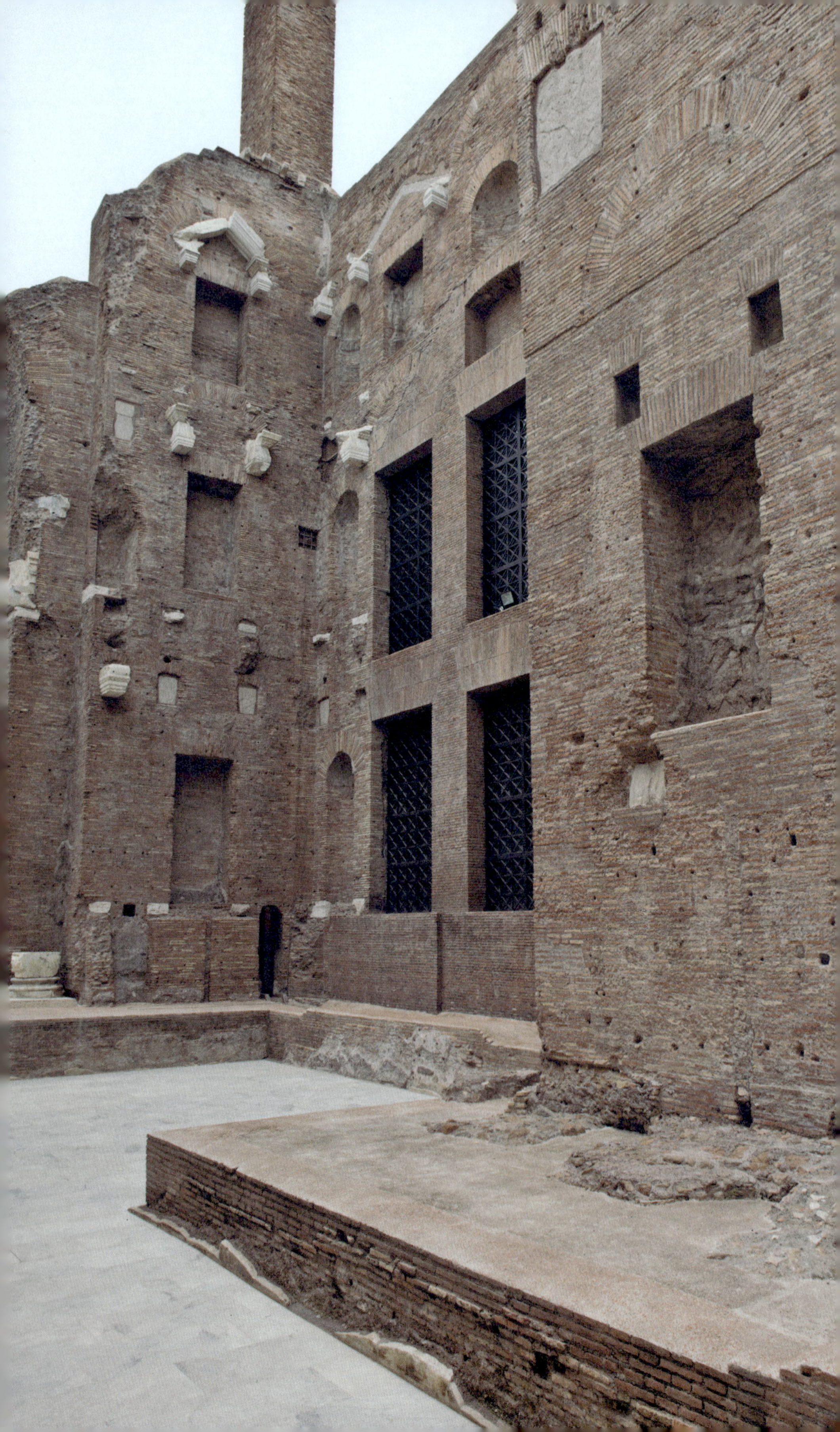

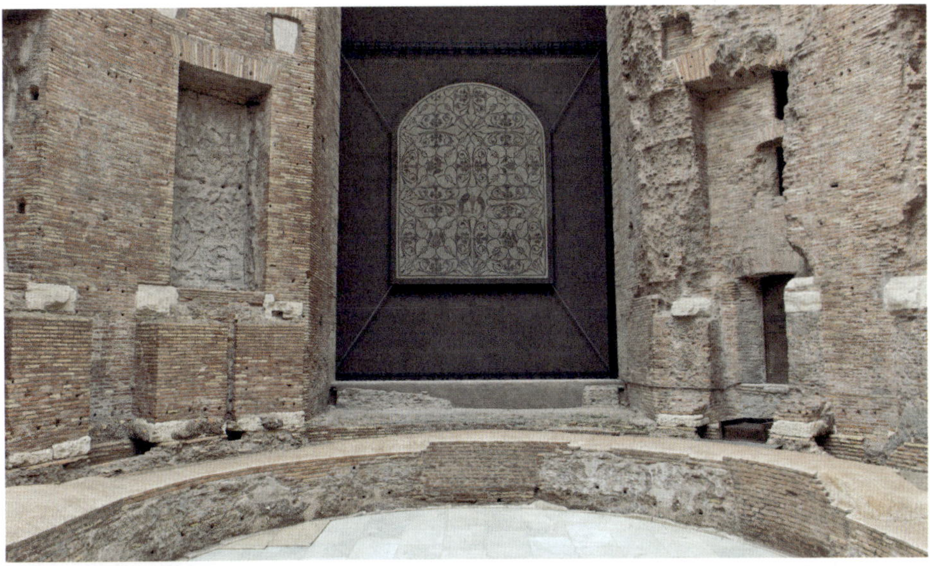

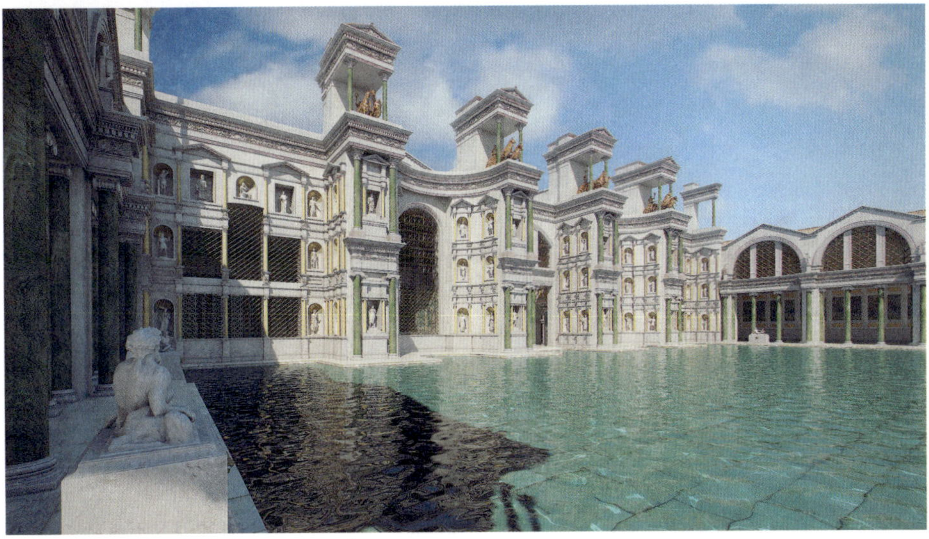

The *natatio*.

Central exedra of the *natatio* with a black-and-white mosaic featuring animal and plant motifs, originating from one of the spaces of the built complex dating from the mid-Imperial period, discovered in Piazza dei Cinquecento during the construction of the first railway station and underground.

3D reconstruction inspired by 19th-century watercolours by Edmond Paulin. Produced by Capware – Technology for Culture.

Hall X.

Hall X

Hall X houses some important funerary monuments. It was probably originally used as an atrium providing access to Hall IX, once an *apodyterium* (changing room). On the left as you enter stands the massive structure from the Julio-Claudian period known as the Tomb of the Platorini, discovered on the right bank of the Tiber in 1880 and reconstructed for the Archaeological Exhibition of 1911. The tomb is preceded by the statues found inside it: the one of a man in heroic nudity, traditionally identified as G. Sulpicius Platorinus, may actually be a portrait of Marcus Artorius Geminus, the probable builder of the tomb around 20 AD, while the statue of a woman may be of its last owner, Antonia Furnilla, who lived in Nero's reign. Inside the cinerary urns have been put back in the places where they were found. The fine bust of Minatia Polla, Artorius Geminus's wife also comes from the tomb. On the opposite side of the hall are the two chamber tombs uncovered in 1951 in the area of the large necropolis on the Via Portuensis and transferred to the Museo Nazionale Romano after a complex intervention to cut them out of the tuff in which they were carved. One tomb has a rich painted decoration (see p. 60), while the other, dated to the beginning of the 3rd century AD, is adorned with extremely refined stuccoes. The small chamber, enlivened by niches and roofed with a tunnel vault, contained a set of decorations with an allegorical meaning, characterized by mythological figures set in the medallions of the vault (Dioscuri, satyrs, nymphs and erotes). The opposite wall is adorned instead with two erotes, floral motifs and a *syrinx*, the wind instrument played by shepherds. Also on display in the hall are several funeral statues, located in the niches, a number of sarcophagi arranged along the walls, including the beautiful one representing the myth of Dionysius and Ariadne found on the Via Labicana. Standing out, finally, for its rarity is the smaller than life-size equestrian statue of a boy that is one of the few examples of the use of one of the most prestigious types of Roman statuary for the burial of a child. (M.C.)

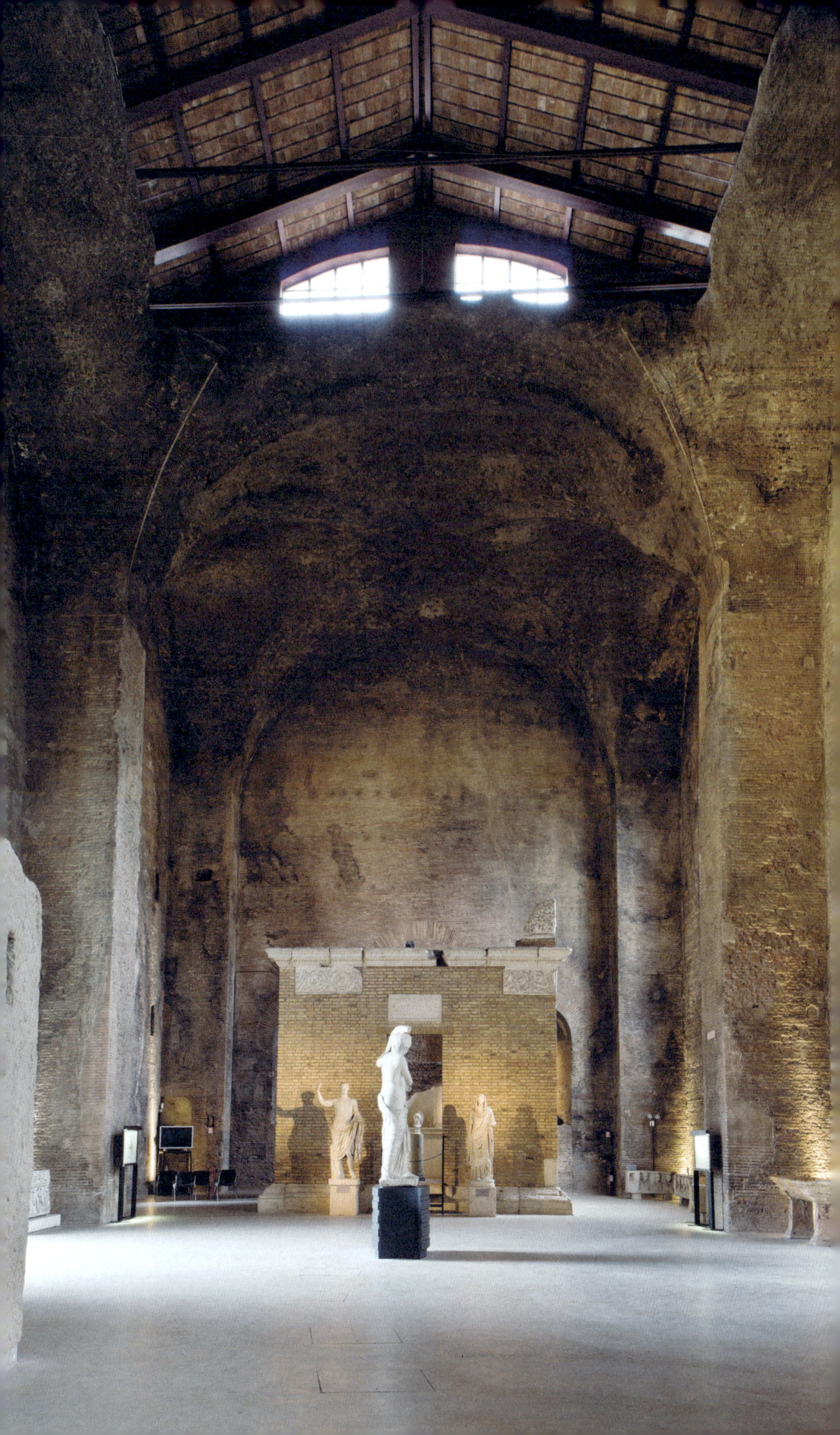

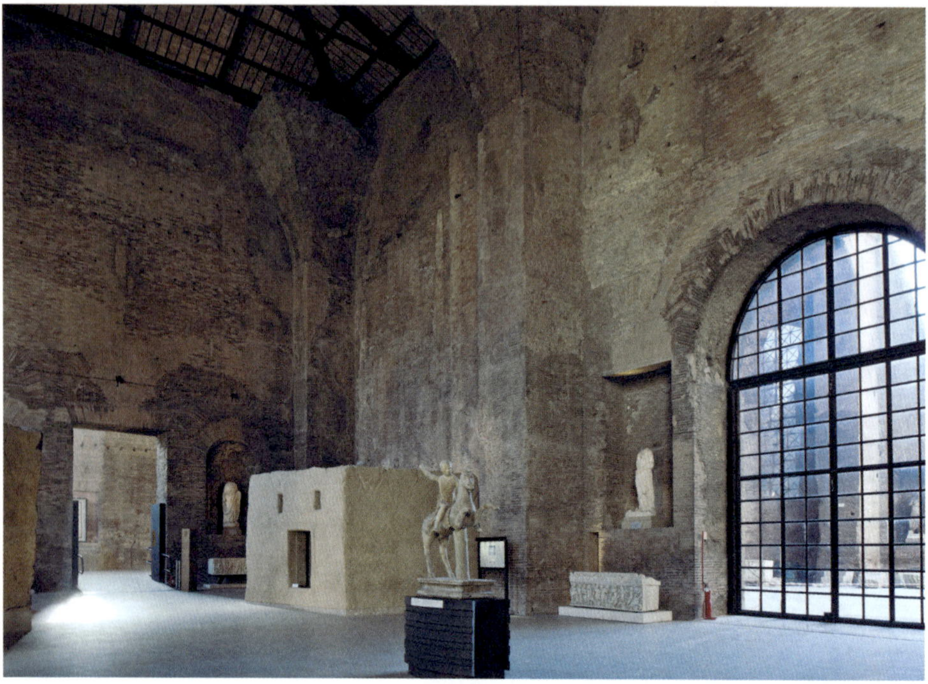

Hall X.

Statue of man in heroic nudity, probably representing M. Artorius Geminus.

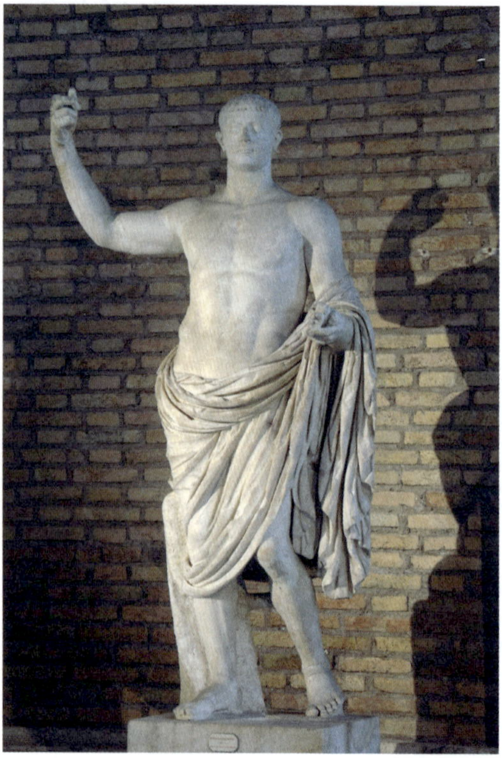

The Painted Tomb from the Via Portuensis

The tomb, carved in tuff and with an approximately rectangular plan, must have belonged to a well-to-do family that used it together with their freedmen. In fact it has a total of 26 niches for the ashes of the cremated in the walls and six spaces for interments. Its painted decoration diverges from the more customary choices in 2nd-century-AD tombs, in which the preference was to rely on the allegorical meaning of mythological scenes as a defense against death. In the decoration of the tomb from the Via Portuensis, dating from around the middle of the century, a more "popular" approach was taken in which symbolic significance was assigned to images drawn from everyday life. In the two lateral tympana of the central wall are set portraits of two young men inserted in medallions, while at bottom right we see a seated couple, probably the parents of the two youths who had died before their time. On the entrance wall is set a scene of a conjugal banquet, while on the ceiling we can recognize the seasons and a scene of a boat landing on a shore; on the left-hand wall three rows of niches are surmounted a pair of peacocks facing one another. In the middle of the wall on the right, devoid of niches, is located the oldest part of the decorative program: here in fact we can see, from the right and under two garlands, three groups of young adults (men and women) playing games: two pairs of men and women engaged excitedly in a ballgame, a youth covering his eyes while a companion flees and a woman seems be holding him back (perhaps it is a game of hide-and-seek rather than blind-man's-buff, in which a blindfold is worn) and finally more young people are seated or lying down, engaged in pleasant conversation or in another game. On the left advances the solitary and out-of-scale figure of a child who is probably learning to walk by playing with a three-wheeled cart. It is likely that the at once familiar and playful scenes on this wall expressed the hope that the afterlife (in the Elysian Fields?) would carry on in a manner not too different from the happy and carefree moments in everyday life, perfectly embodied by this little "catalogue" of games, played by children and grownups. If, however, the child depicted on his own was the deceased commemorated, then they may also have been an allusion to the joys denied him by the brevity of his life. (M.C.)

Frescoes of people playing games from a painted tomb on the Via Portuensis.

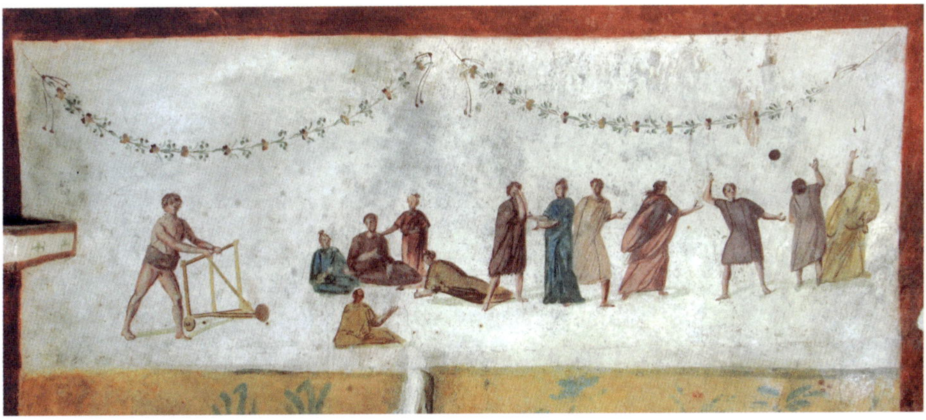

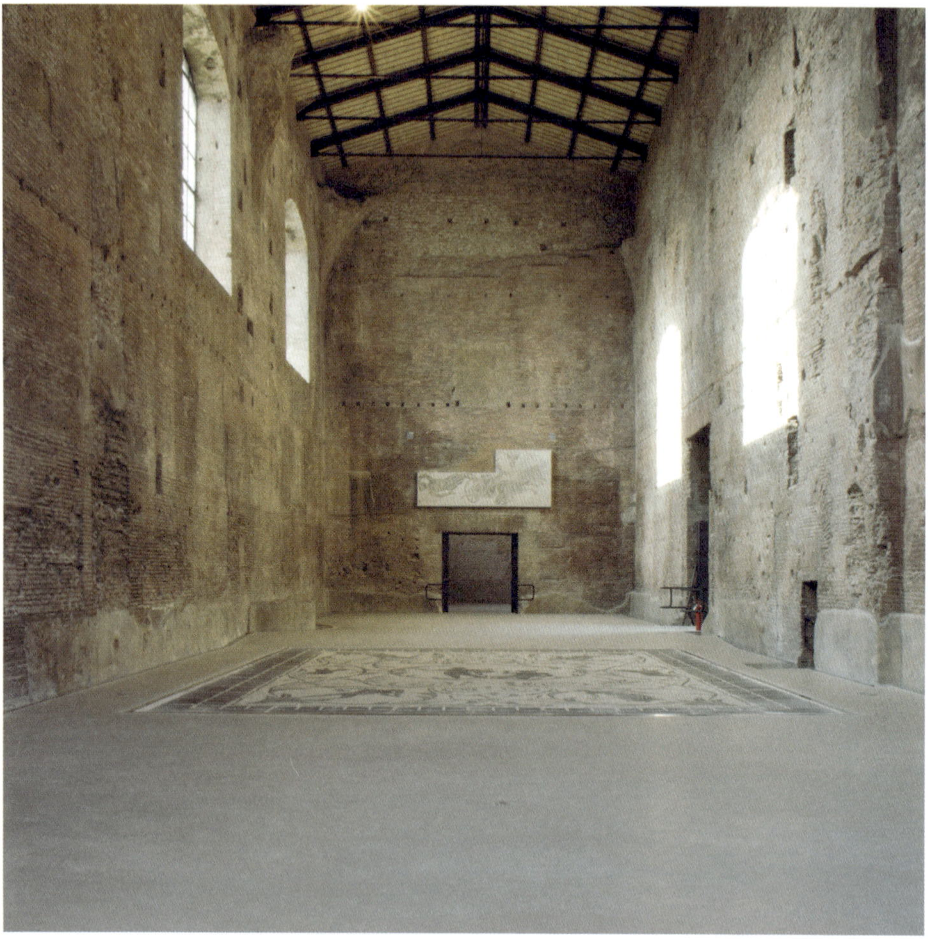

Hall XI; at the back, the passage leading to Hall XI B.

Hall XI

This large hall (measuring 40 x 10 metres) was covered by a long barrel vault. The hall was used as a water storage for the huge open air annexed pool, the *natatio*. The doors were closed with half-round buttresses and the walls were covered by waterproof plaster until a hight of five meters.

In the middle of the hall, there is the great floor mosaic originating from the so-called Nero's Villa in Antium: in the centre, inside a fine foliage design, Hercules, recognisable by the club and by the lion's skin, holds the horn he tore off the bleeding head of the river god Achelous, defeated in the contest for the hand of the princess Deianira. On the left wall there is the mosaic coming from a funerary area and depicting a human skeleton reclined on a symposium couch. He is pointing to the Delphic Oracle's motto *Gnothi sauton*, "know yourself", the exhortation to know the limits of human nature and the brevity of earthly existence. The mosaic fragment found in a wealthy residence in Ceccano can be found on the back wall of the hall.

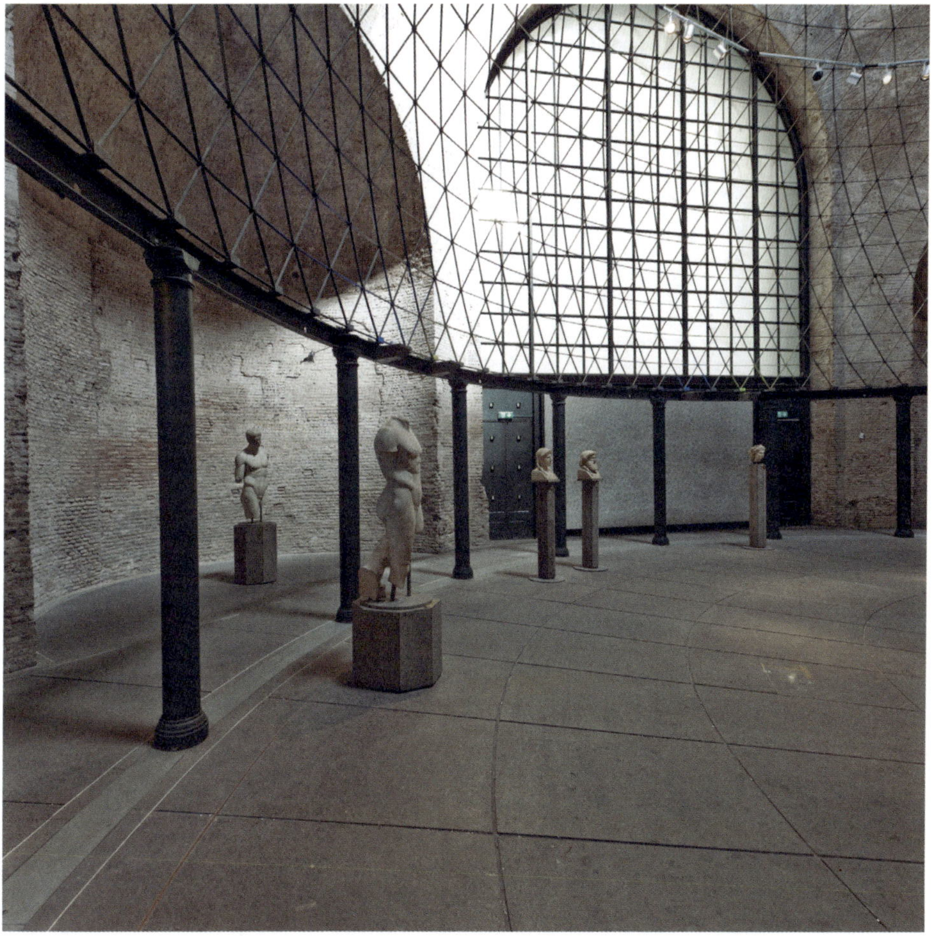

View of the interior of the Octagonal Hall with sculptures from thermal baths.

It depicts an episode of the Trojan War narrated in Virgil's *Aeneid*: the young Trojan prince Troilus, one of the sons of the King Priamus, stabbed by Achilles, hangs from his chariot, his spear scribbling in the dust, while his horses flee. In the upper part another male figure is depicted, probably Achilles, armed with a spear. (C. B.)

The Octagonal Hall

The Octagonal Hall is part of the central complex of the Baths of Diocletian and the last of the four rooms that were located next to the *caldarium* and that were converted into a store for Rome's grain supply in 1575, eventually becoming, in 1764, part of the storehouses for oil (the "Olearie"). The first two halls also survive in part and now house the Faculty of Education, while Via Cernaia cuts through the third. The fourth hall is square on the outside and octagonal on the inside (with semicircular niches in the corners) and may have been used as the baths' secondary *frigidarium*, judging by the fact that it contained a hexagonal basin up until the 16th century. The present

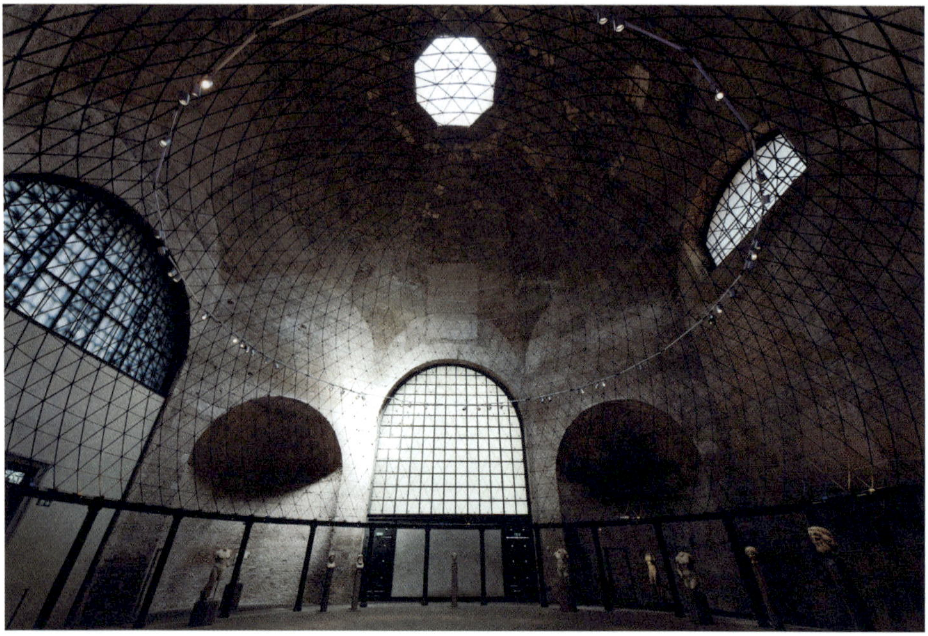

View of the interior of the Octagonal Hall with sculptures from thermal baths.

floor is the result of the papal interventions that subdivided the hall into three stories. The "umbrella" dome is still the original one, while the stucco decoration of the ceiling and the marble decoration of the walls have been lost. The hall was used for the great Archaeological Exhibition of 1911, but then turned first into a cinema (Sala Minerva) and then a planetarium (1928), the largest in Europe at the time. It was not until 1991 that the building was restructured and used to display sculptures found in baths, in order to give these works back their original function in a similar setting to the one for which they were intended. Today it is used for exhibitions as well. The statues on show also give us an idea of the subjects portrayed in baths, chiefly images of athletes, heroes and deities. They formed complex decorative programmes that unfortunately cannot be reconstructed today. Among the statues from the Baths of Diocletian themselves it is worth mentioning the copy of Praxiteles's *Aphrodite of Cnidus*, a remarkable man's torso, copy of a classical original, and the beautiful head of a young athlete from the time of Hadrian, copy of an original in the severe style. From the Baths of Caracalla come two copies of works by Polyclitus (a torso of the *Doryphorus* and the statue of *Heracles*) and a fine statue of *Aphrodite Anadyomene* ("Rising From the Sea"), shown wringing the water from her hair, that was found in the Mithraeum under the baths. Several heads, like that of Asclepius and one of a youth wearing a diadem, also come from Caracalla's Baths, while a pair of herms of Apollo and Hermes probably decorated their library. Finally a copy of Praxiteles's *Lycian Apollo* was found in the Baths of Trajan. (M.C.)

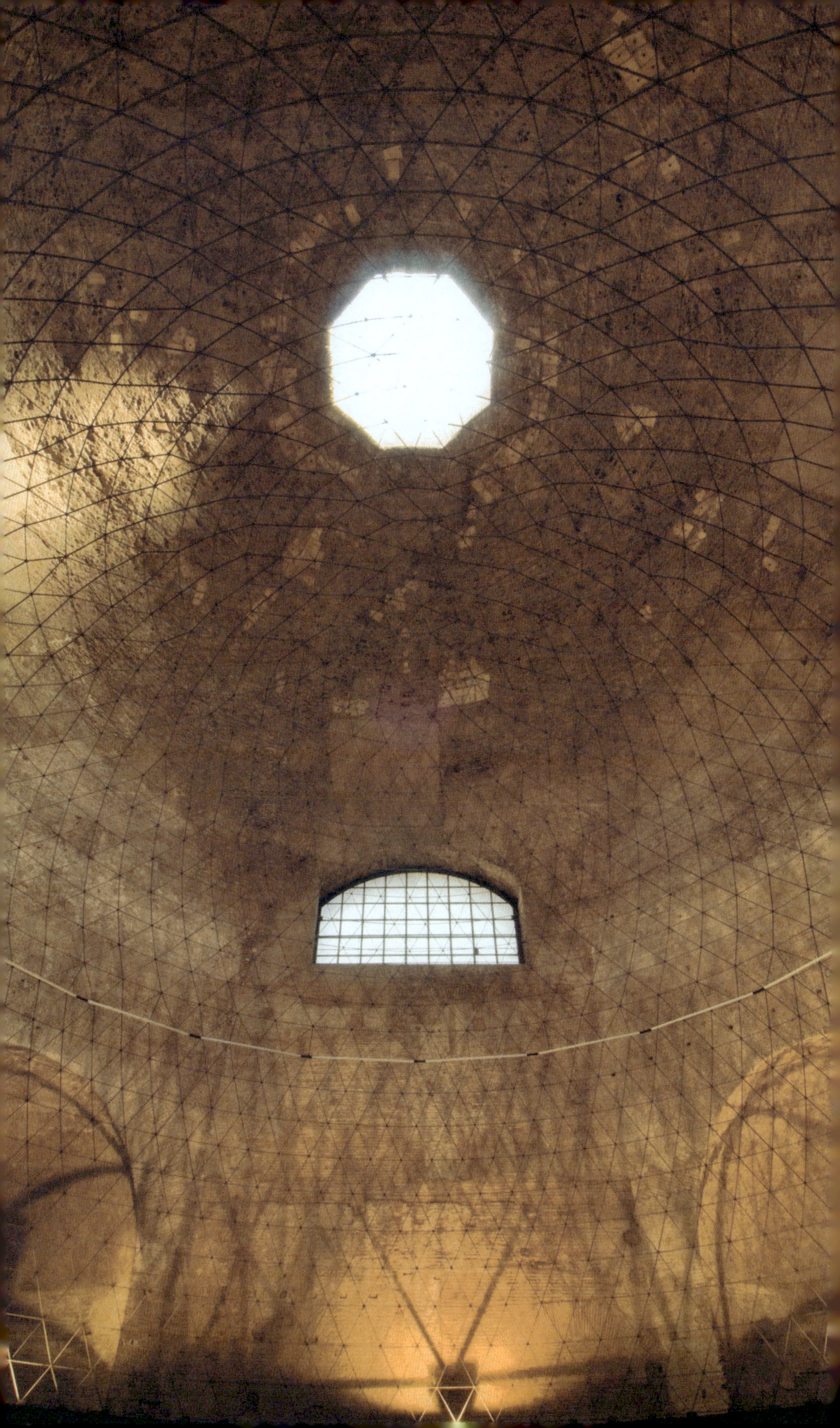

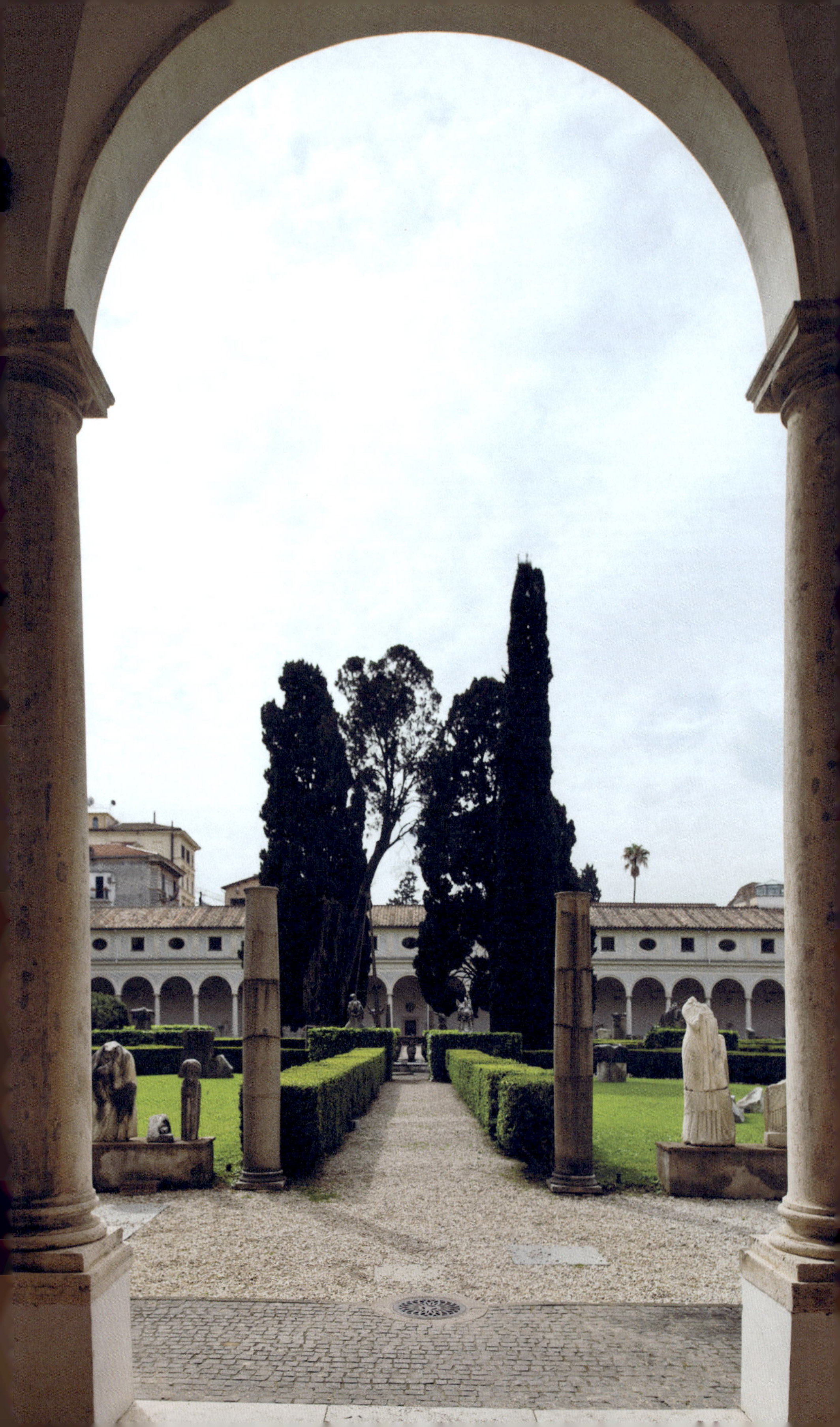

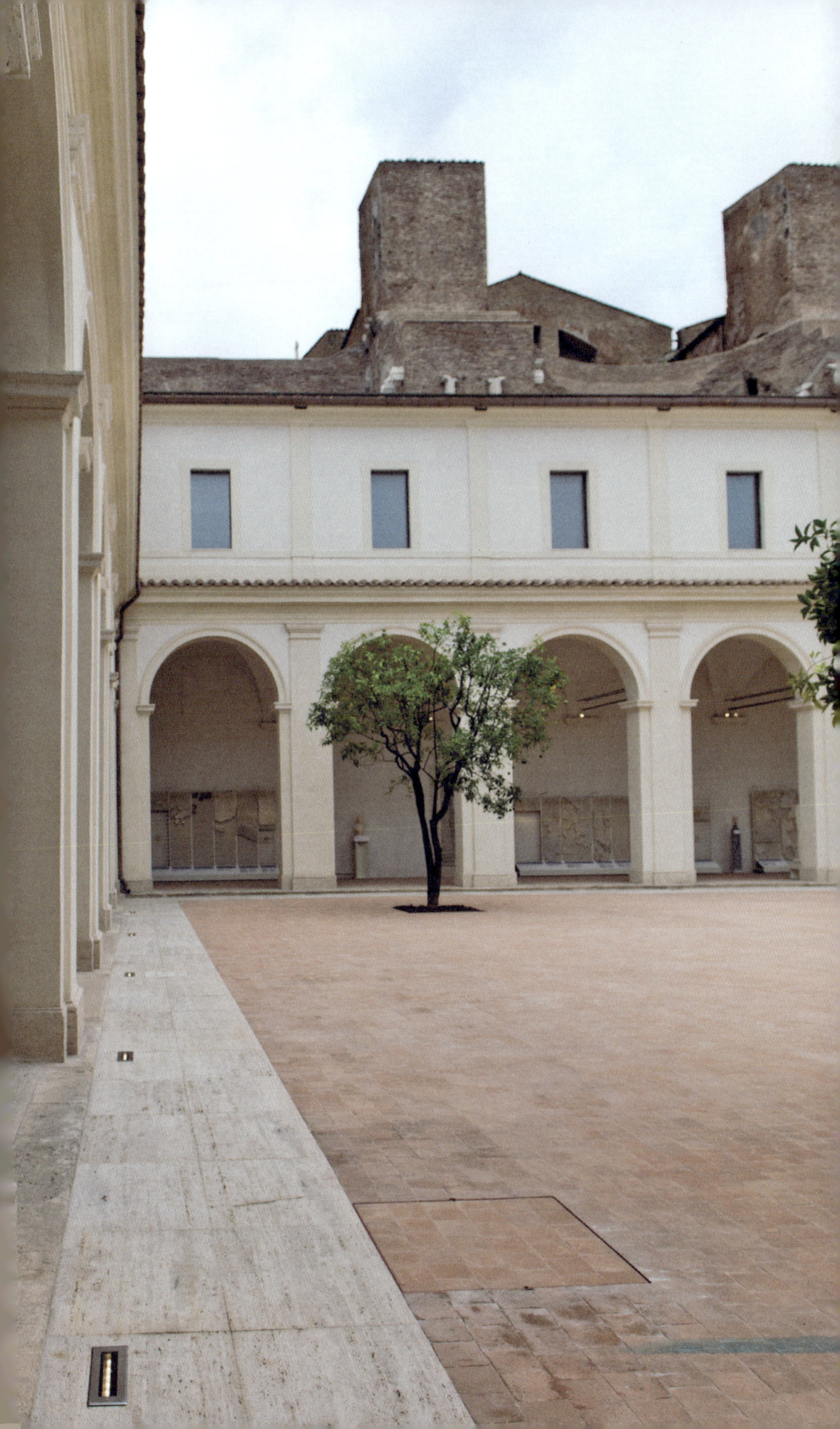

Bibliography

N. Horsfall, *CIL VI 37965 = CLE 1988 Epitaph of Allia Potestas: a commentary*, in "ZPE", 1985, pp. 251-272.

F. Silvestrini, *Sepulcrum Marci Artori Gemini. La tomba detta dei Platorini nel Museo Nazionale Romano*, Roma 1987.

M. Rita Sanzi di Mino (ed. by), *Rotunda Diocletiani. Sculture decorative delle terme nel Museo Nazionale Romano*, Roma 1991.

L. Nista (ed. by), *Sacellum Herculis. Le sculture del tempio di Ercole a Trastevere*, Roma 1991.

Fidene. Una casa dell'età del ferro, Milano 1998.

S. De Maria, *Le tombeau de la via Portuense à Rome*, in N. Blanc (ed. by), *Au royaume des ombres. La peinture funéraire antique* (exhibition catalogue, Saint-Romain-en-Gal, Vienne 1998), Paris 1998, pp. 126-130.

A.M. Bietti Sestieri, A. De Santis, *Protostoria dei popoli latini: Museo nazionale romano, Terme di Diocleziano*, Milano 2000.

R. Friggeri, *La collezione epigrafica del Museo Nazionale Romano alle Terme di Diocleziano*, Milano 2001.

Museo Nazionale Romano. Terme di Diocleziano, Milano 2002.

R. Friggeri, M.G. Granino Cecere, G.L. Gregori (ed. by), *Terme di Diocleziano. La collezione epigrafica*, Milano 2012.

R. Friggeri, M.Magnani Cianetti con C. Caruso (ed. by), *Terme di Diocleziano. Il Chiostro piccolo della Certosa di Santa Maria degli Angeli*, Milano 2014.

Cover and graphics
Tassinari/Vetta

Translations
Antony Bowden
Christopher Evans

This volume was printed
for Mondadori Electa S.p.A.
by Elcograf S.p.A., Via Mondadori, 15
Verona, in 2019